Practice B
the WISC®-V Test

Improve

Nonverbal

and

Processing Speed

Skills with 180

Exercises

Zoe Hampton

Other IQ books by the author
https://prfc.nl/go/amznbooks

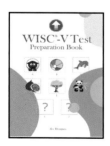

Our Mobile Applications for IQ Training

https://prfc.nl/go/allapps

Our IQ Cubes

The box contains 9 pieces of IQ Cubes

Order link: https://prfc.nl/go/amzniqcubes

Follow us on social media

Web site: https://prfc.nl/go/pc

Facebook: https://prfc.nl/go/fbpc

Instagram: https://prfc.nl/go/inpc

LinkedIn: https://prfc.nl/go/lipc

YouTube: https://prfc.nl/go/ytpc

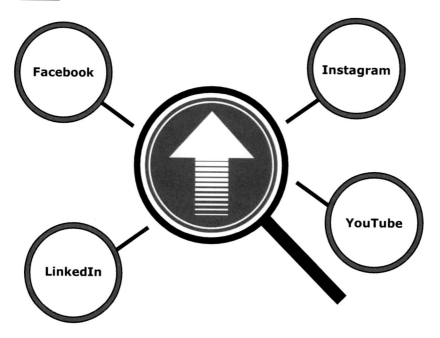

Table of Contents

Introduction

Practice Book for the WISC®-V Test

Wechsler Intelligence Scale for Children/WISC® is used to assess intelligence in children between the ages of 6 to 16 years old. It's made up of 16 primary subtests and five com-plementary subtests. The WISC®-V test takes between 50 and 65 minutes to administer. The purpose of the test is to find out if the child is gifted or not, and to determine the stu-dent's cognitive strengths and weaknesses.

This practice book contains also two of the new primary sub-tests: Visual puzzles and Figure Weights.

About this book

This practice book consists of 180 exercises. They will help to improve the solving skills of WISC®-V test. The exercises are non-verbal and are suitable for children of all language groups. The book contains exercises from the following sub-tests:

- Visual Puzzles
- Matrix Reasoning
- Figure Weights
- Coding
- Symbol Search
- Cancellation
- Block Design

Visual Puzzles

Visual Puzzles is a new WISC-V subtest. There are 20 questions of this type in this practice book. During the real test, the child must answer the questions within a certain time. In each question there is a complete puzzle, the child must choose three of the answers so that they form the indicated puzzle. The questions start with easier ones and gradually become more difficult. Success!

Notice: In the given answers, the parts can be rotated!

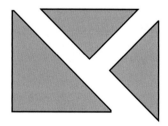

Answer on page 147

Question 1

*Choose the 3 pieces below that combine
to complete the shape above*

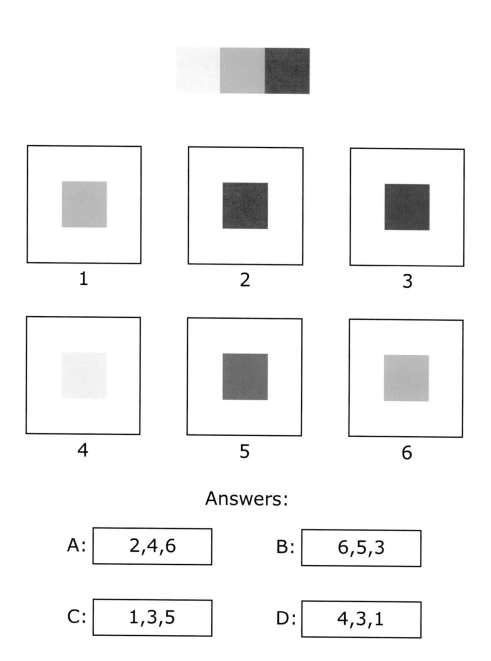

Answers:

A: 2,4,6   B: 6,5,3

C: 1,3,5   D: 4,3,1

Question 2

*Choose the 3 pieces below that combine
to complete the shape above*

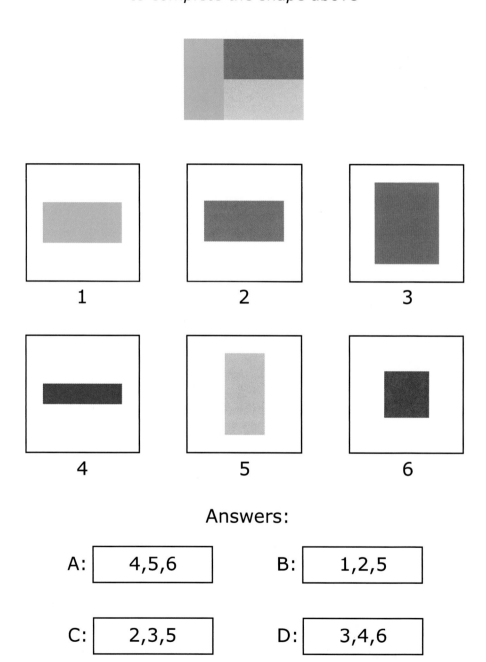

Answers:

A: 4,5,6   B: 1,2,5

C: 2,3,5   D: 3,4,6

Question 3

*Choose the 3 pieces below that combine
to complete the shape above*

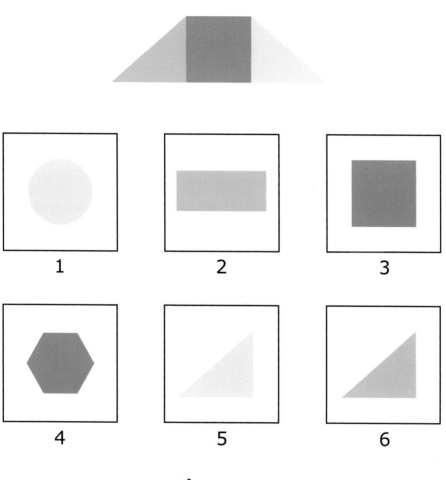

Answers:

A: | 1,3,5 |

B: | 4,2,6 |

C: | 3,5,6 |

D: | 4,1,2 |

Answer on page 147

Question 4

*Choose the 3 pieces below that combine
to complete the shape above*

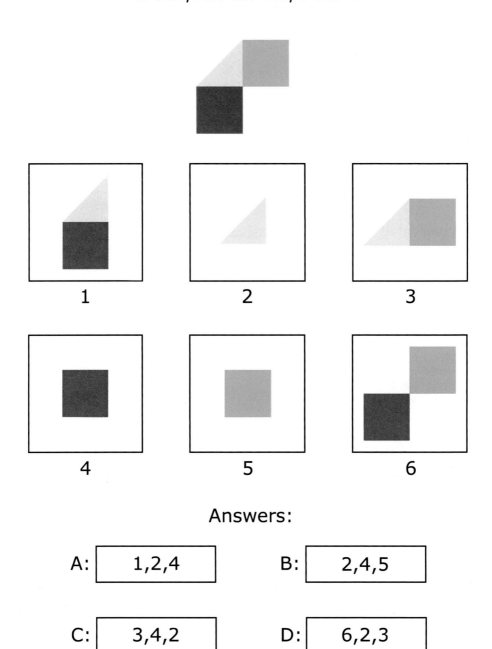

1

2

3

4

5

6

Answers:

A: 1,2,4

B: 2,4,5

C: 3,4,2

D: 6,2,3

Question 5

Choose the 3 pieces below that combine
to complete the shape above

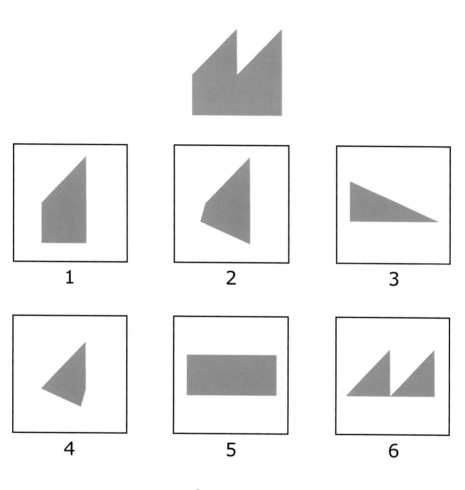

Answers:

A: 3,5,6

B: 1,5,6

C: 1,4,5

D: 2,3,4

Question 6

*Choose the 3 pieces below that combine
to complete the shape above*

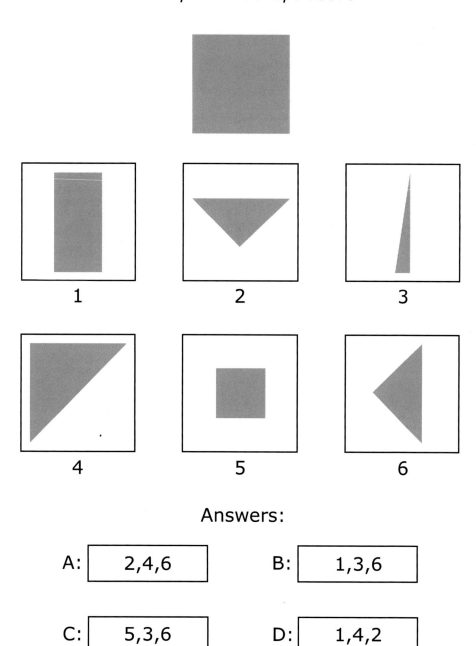

Answers:

A: | 2,4,6

B: | 1,3,6

C: | 5,3,6

D: | 1,4,2

Question 7

*Choose the 3 pieces below that combine
to complete the shape above*

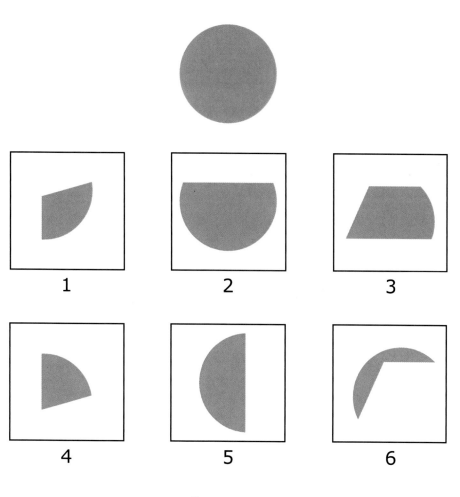

1

2

3

4

5

6

Answers:

A: | 1,3,6

B: | 3,5,6

C: | 1,4,5

D: | 2,5,4

Answer on page 147

Question 8

*Choose the 3 pieces below that combine
to complete the shape above*

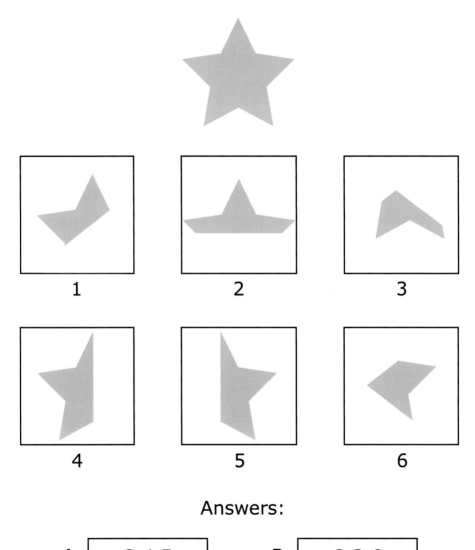

Answers:

A: 2,4,5

B: 2,3,6

C: 1,3,6

D: 1,2,5

Answer on page 147

Question 9

*Choose the 3 pieces below that combine
to complete the shape above*

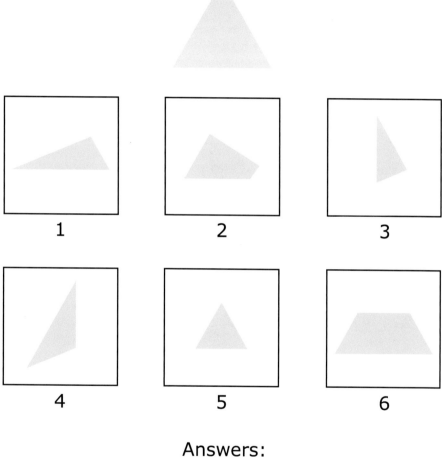

1

2

3

4

5

6

Answers:

A: | 2,5,4

B: | 1,3,4

C: | 5,6,3

D: | 2,3,4

Question 10

*Choose the 3 pieces below that combine
to complete the shape above*

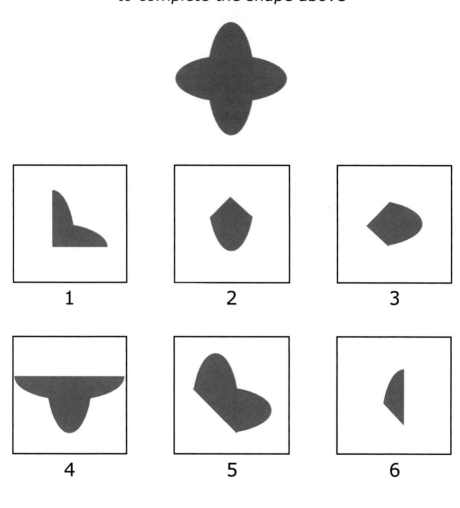

1

2

3

4

5

6

Answers:

A: | 1,4,6

B: | 3,4,5

C: | 2,3,5

D: | 2,5,6

Question 11

*Choose the 3 pieces below that combine
to complete the shape above*

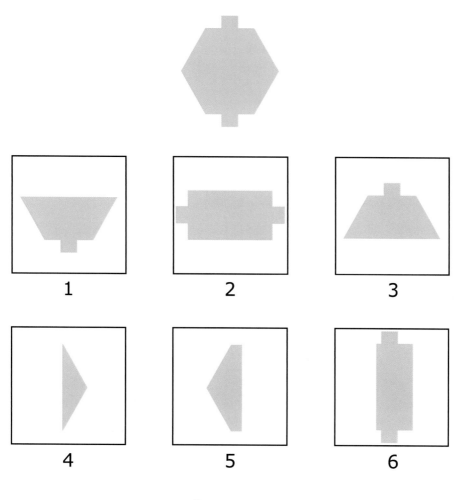

Answers:

A: | 2,4,5   B: | 1,3,4

C: | 3,5,6   D: | 4,5,6

Answer on page 147

Question 12

*Choose the 3 pieces below that combine
to complete the shape above*

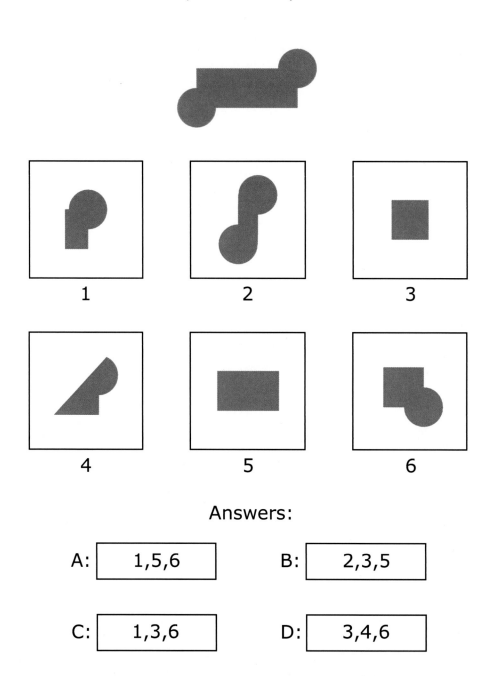

1

2

3

4

5

6

Answers:

A: | 1,5,6

B: | 2,3,5

C: | 1,3,6

D: | 3,4,6

Question 13

*Choose the 3 pieces below that combine
to complete the shape above*

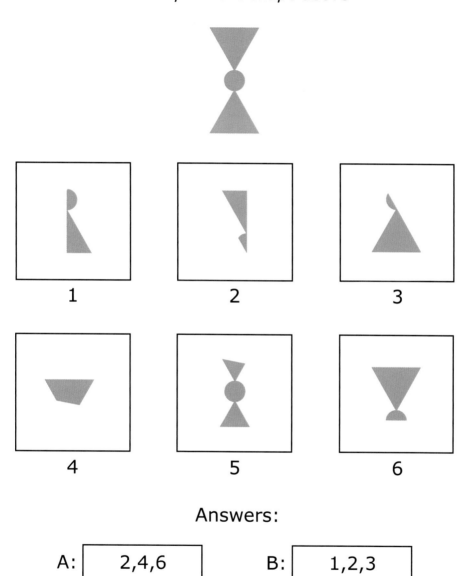

1

2

3

4

5

6

Answers:

A: 2,4,6

B: 1,2,3

C: 2,3,4

D: 1,2,6

Question 14

*Choose the 3 pieces below that combine
to complete the shape above*

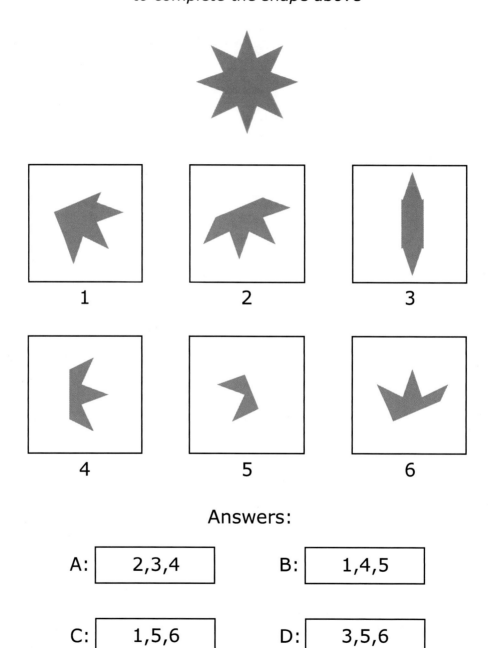

1

2

3

4

5

6

Answers:

A: | 2,3,4

B: | 1,4,5

C: | 1,5,6

D: | 3,5,6

Question 15

*Choose the 3 pieces below that combine
to complete the shape above*

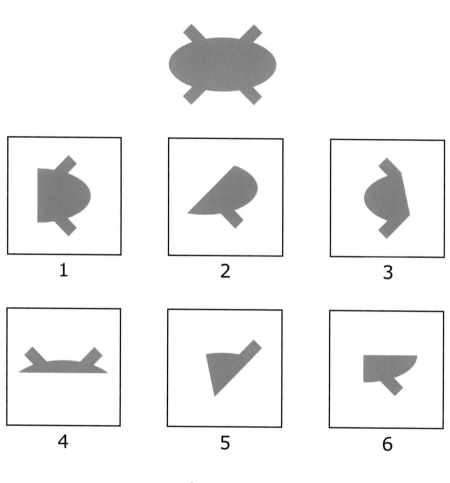

Answers:

A: 1,3,5   B: 2,4,6

C: 4,5,6   D: 2,3,5

Question 16

*Choose the 3 pieces below that combine
to complete the shape above*

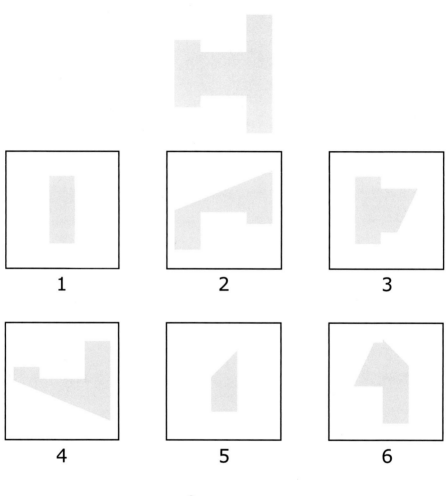

1 2 3

4 5 6

Answers:

A: | 3,5,6

B: | 1,3,6

C: | 2,4,5

D: | 1,2,4

Question 17

*Choose the 3 pieces below that combine
to complete the shape above*

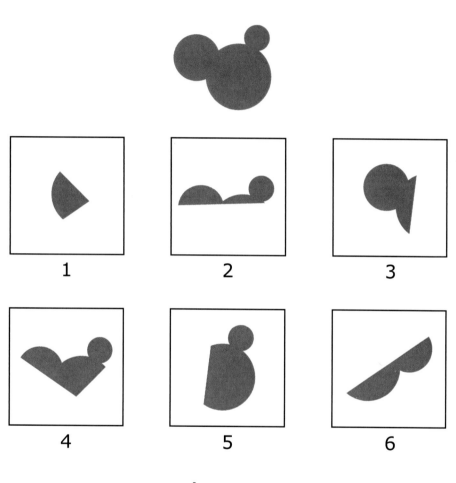

1

2

3

4

5

6

Answers:

A: | 1,2,3

B: | 2,4,5

C: | 2,3,6

D: | 1,4,6

Question 18

Choose the 3 pieces below that combine
to complete the shape above

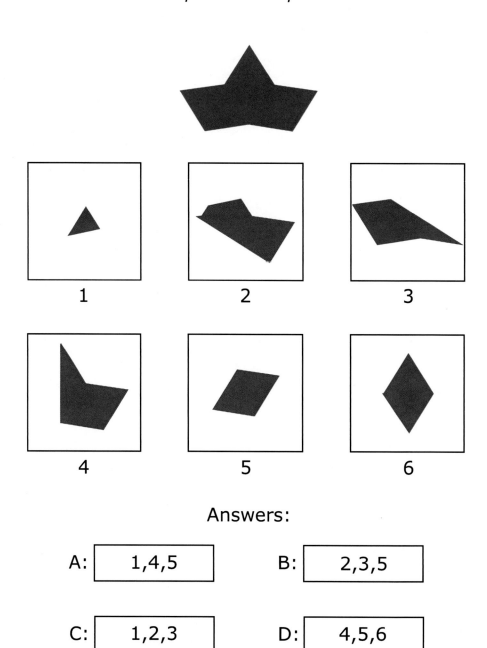

1

2

3

4

5

6

Answers:

A: | 1,4,5

B: | 2,3,5

C: | 1,2,3

D: | 4,5,6

Question 19

*Choose the 3 pieces below that combine
to complete the shape above*

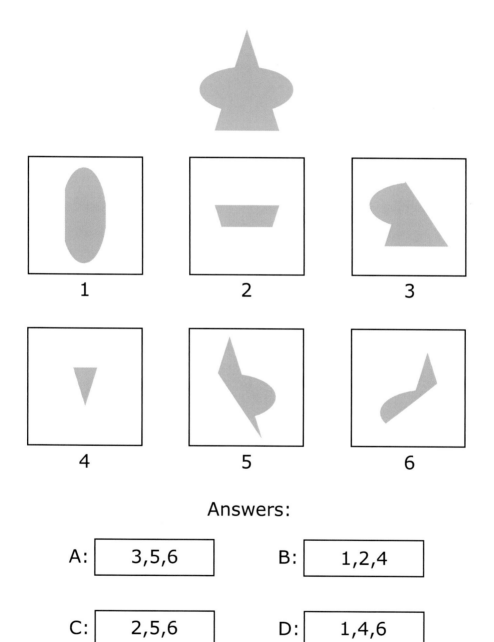

1

2

3

4

5

6

Answers:

A: 3,5,6

B: 1,2,4

C: 2,5,6

D: 1,4,6

Question 20

*Choose the 3 pieces below that combine
to complete the shape above*

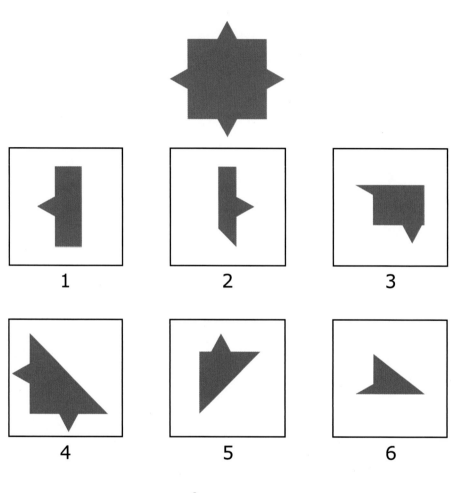

1

2

3

4

5

6

Answers:

A: 2,4,5

B: 1,2,3

C: 3,5,6

D: 1,4,6

Matrix Reasoning

Matrix Reasoning is an untimed Perceptual Reasoning subtest.

The questions of this subtest in this practice book are 40. 20 of them are matrix questions and the other 20 are pattern questions. The child is shown colored matrices or visual patterns in which something is missing. The child is asked to select the missing piece from a set of options so that the matrix or specified pattern is completed.

The questions start with easier ones and gradually become more difficult.

Success!

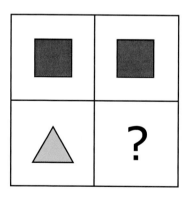

Answer on page 148

Question 21

*Which of the following images completes
the missing part?*

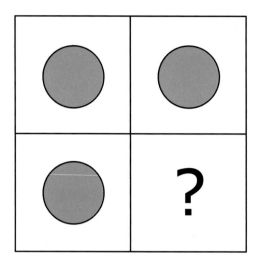

Answers:

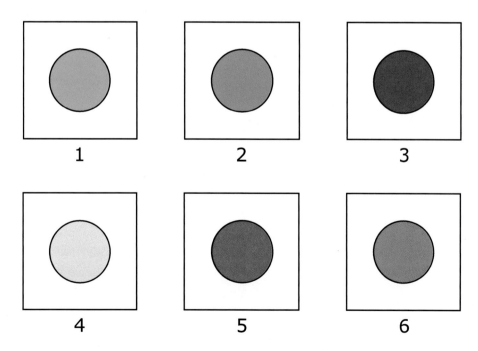

Answer on page 148

Question 22

Which of the following images completes the missing part?

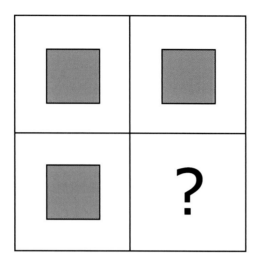

Answers:

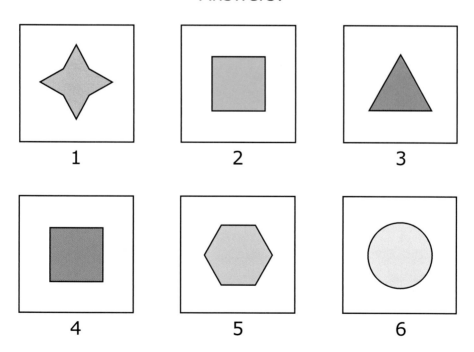

Question 23

Which of the following images completes the missing part?

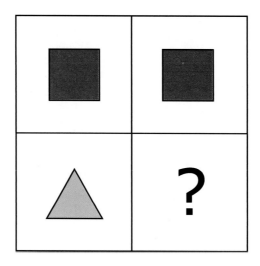

Answers:

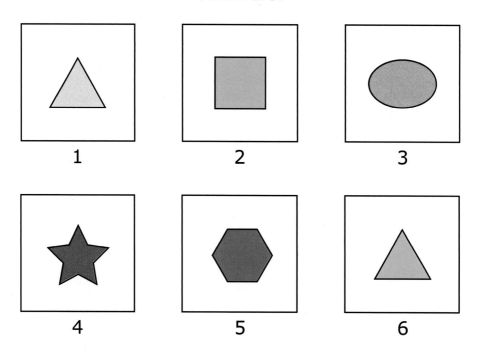

Question 24

*Which of the following images completes
the missing part?*

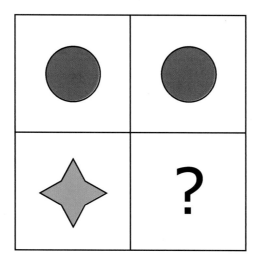

Answers:

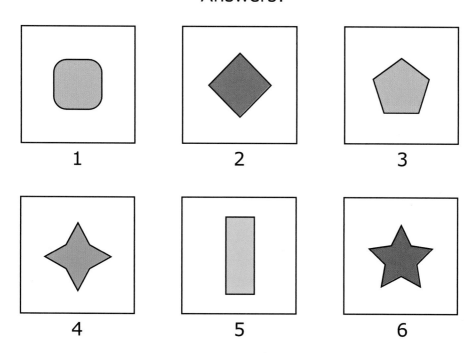

Question 25

*Which of the following images completes
the missing part?*

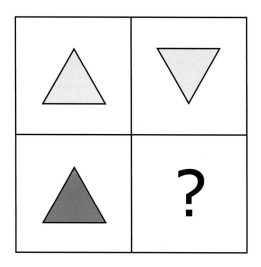

Answers:

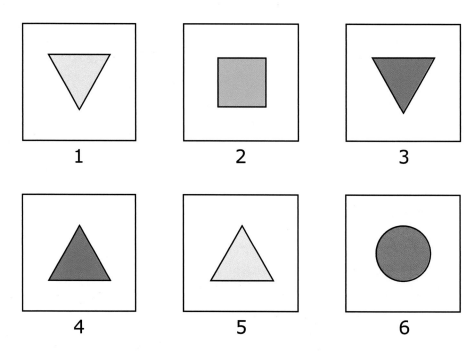

Question 26

*Which of the following images completes
the missing part?*

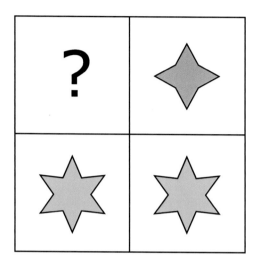

Answers:

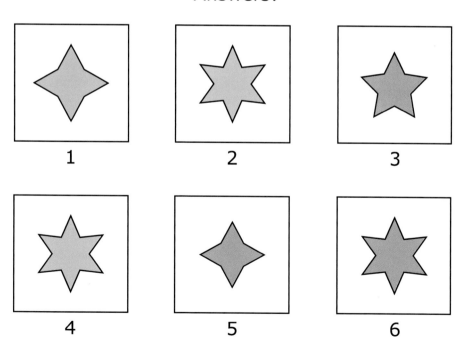

1   2   3

4   5   6

Answer on page 148

Question 27

*Which of the following images completes
the missing part?*

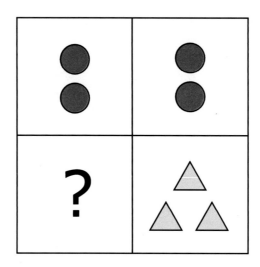

Answers:

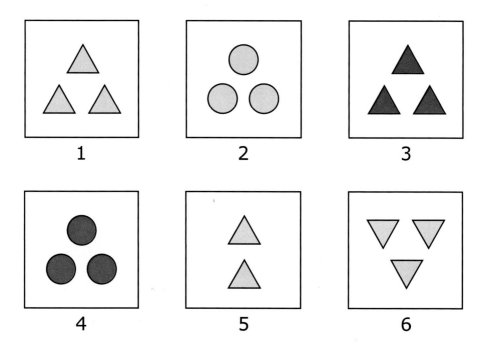

1   2   3

4   5   6

Answer on page 148

Question 28

*Which of the following images completes
the missing part?*

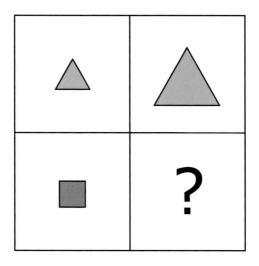

Answers:

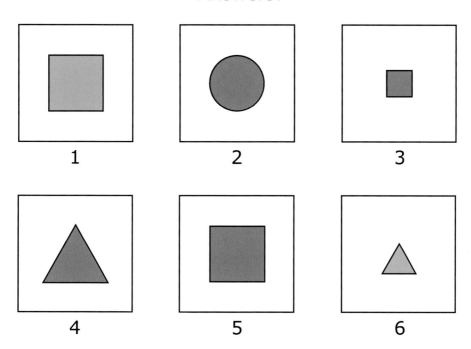

Question 29

Which of the following images completes the missing part?

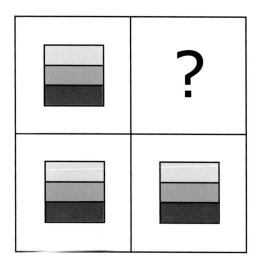

Answers:

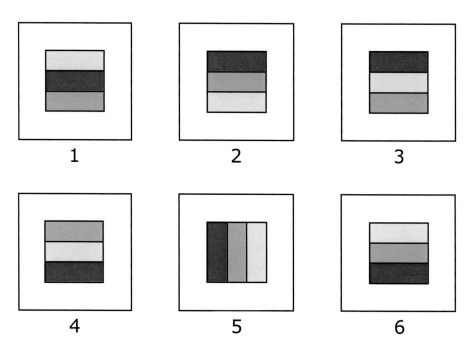

Question 30

*Which of the following images completes
the missing part?*

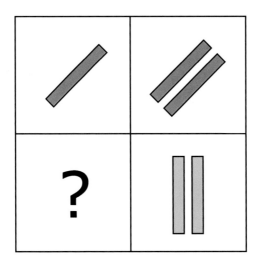

Answers:

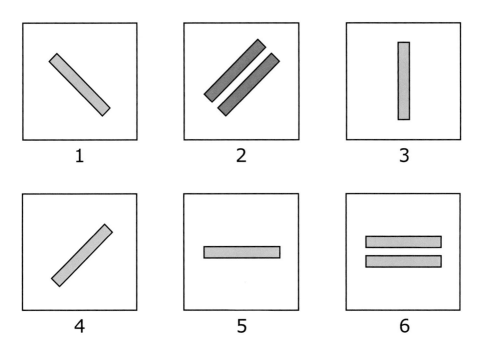

1   2   3

4   5   6

Answer on page 148

Question 31

*Which of the following images completes
the missing part?*

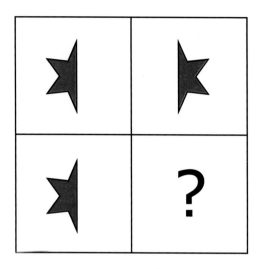

Answers:

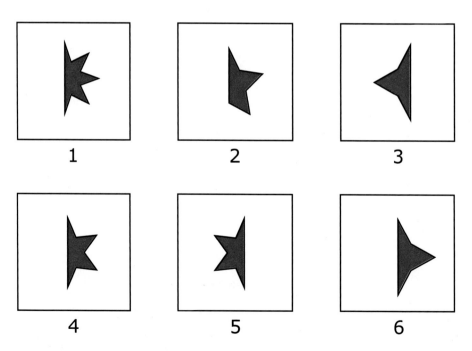

Question 32

Which of the following images completes the missing part?

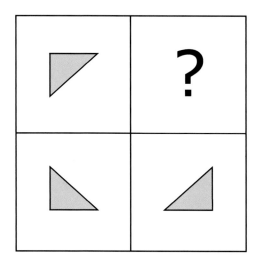

Answers:

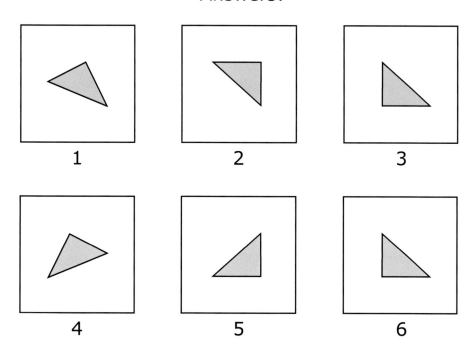

Question 33

*Which of the following images completes
the missing part?*

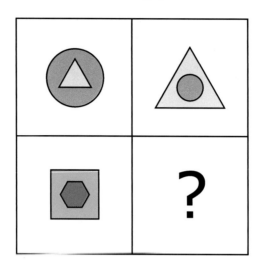

Answers:

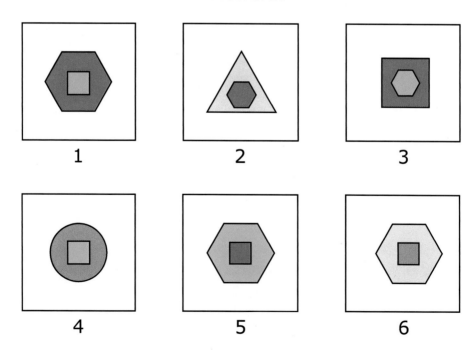

Question 34

*Which of the following images completes
the missing part?*

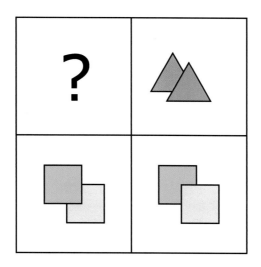

Answers:

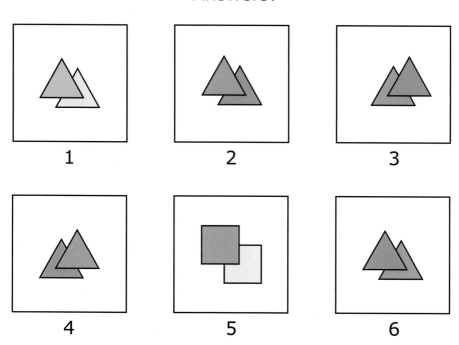

Question 35

*Which of the following images completes
the missing part?*

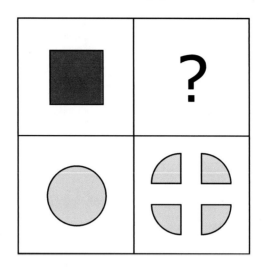

Answers:

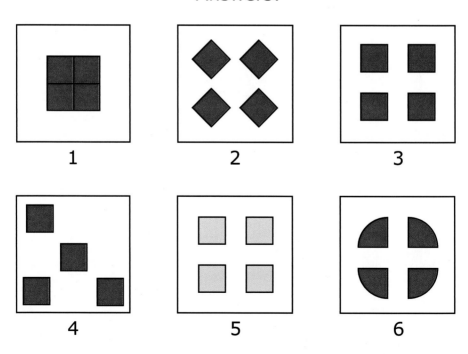

Question 36

Which of the following images completes the missing part?

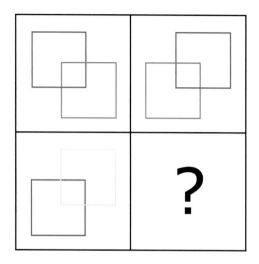

Answers:

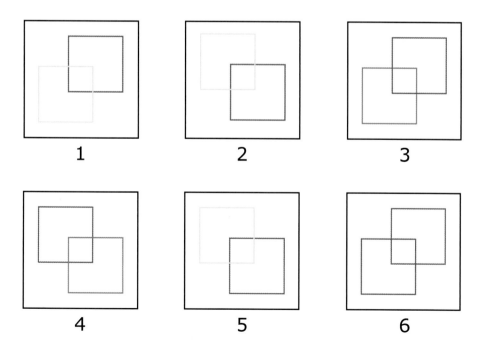

Question 37

*Which of the following images completes
the missing part?*

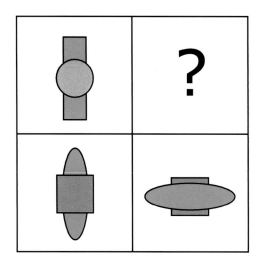

Answers:

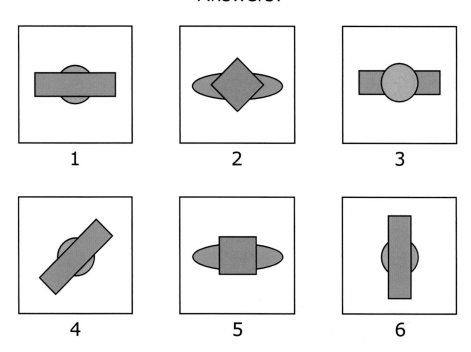

1   2   3

4   5   6

Question 38

*Which of the following images completes
the missing part?*

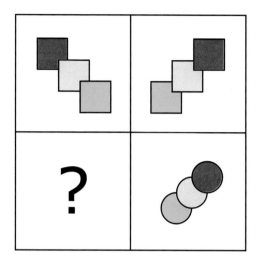

Answers:

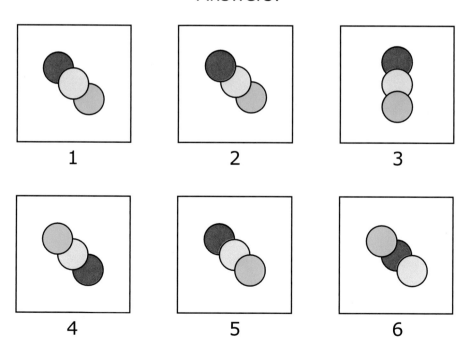

1   2   3

4   5   6

Question 39

*Which of the following images completes
the missing part?*

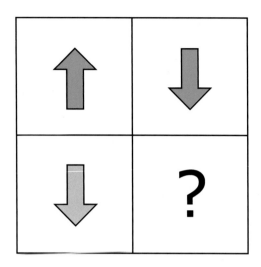

Answers:

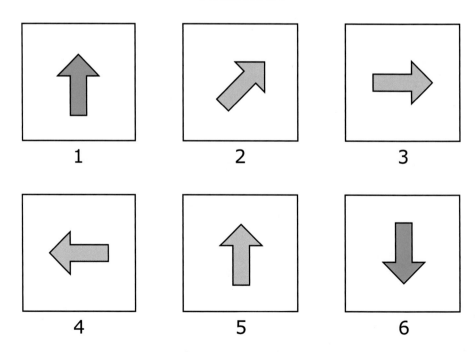

Question 40

*Which of the following images completes
the missing part?*

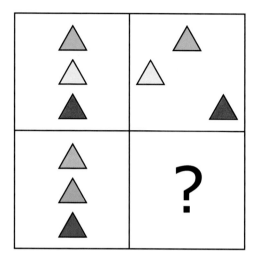

Answers:

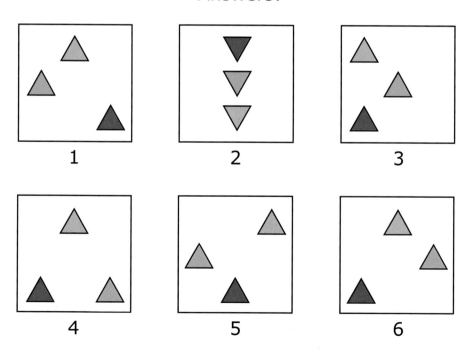

Question 41

What comes next in the pattern?

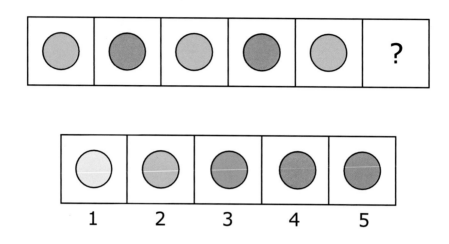

Question 42

What comes next in the pattern?

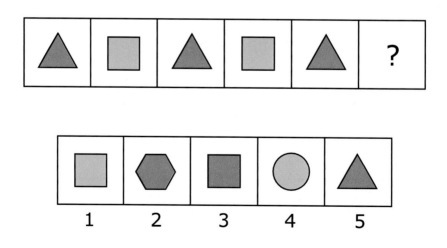

Answer on page 148

Question 43

What comes next in the pattern?

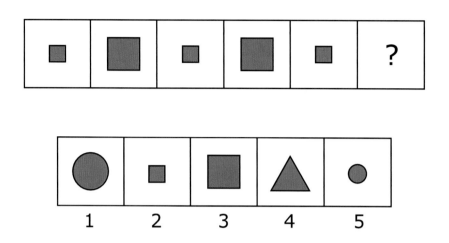

Question 44

What comes next in the pattern?

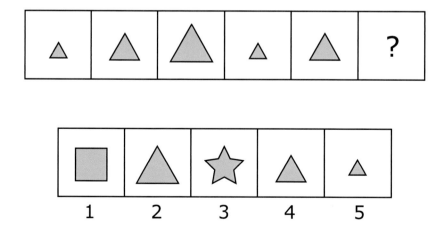

Question 45

What comes next in the pattern?

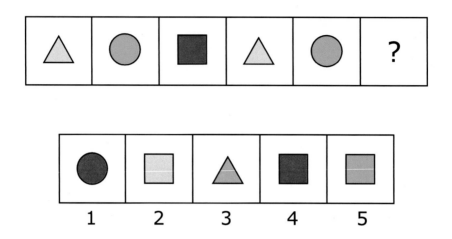

Question 46

What comes next in the pattern?

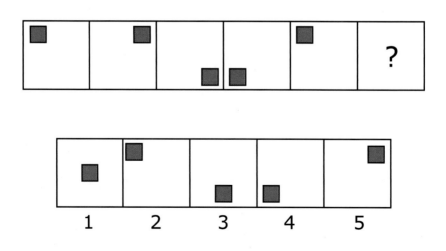

Question 47

What comes next in the pattern?

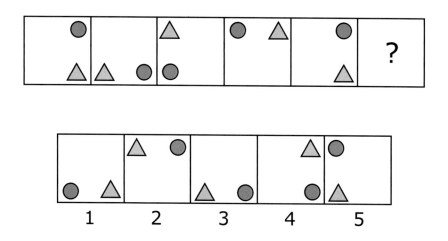

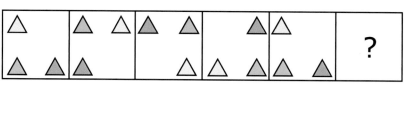

Question 48

What comes next in the pattern?

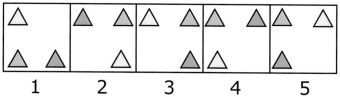

Question 49

What comes next in the pattern?

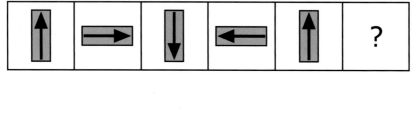

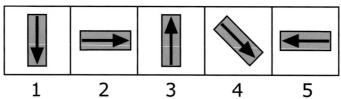

Question 50

What comes next in the pattern?

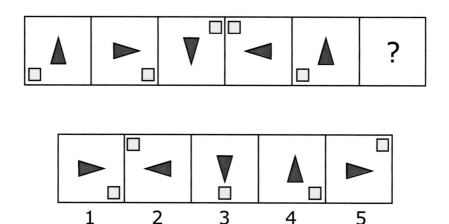

Question 51

What comes next in the pattern?

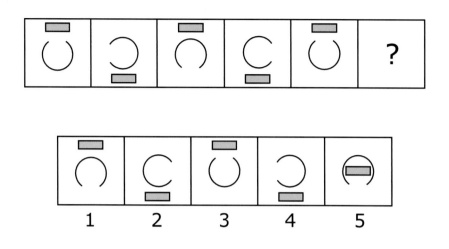

Question 52

What comes next in the pattern?

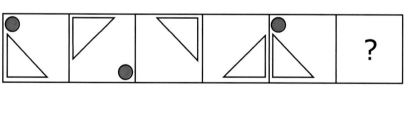

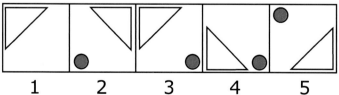

Question 53

What comes next in the pattern?

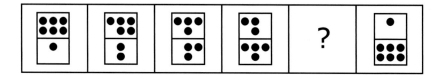

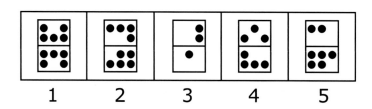

Question 54

What comes next in the pattern?

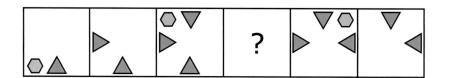

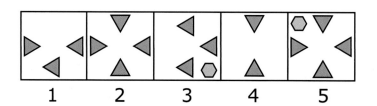

Question 55

What comes next in the pattern?

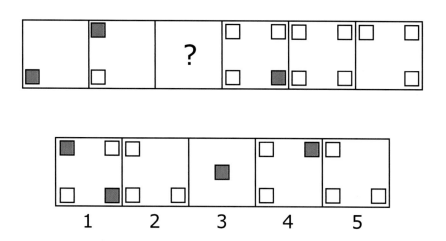

Question 56

What comes next in the pattern?

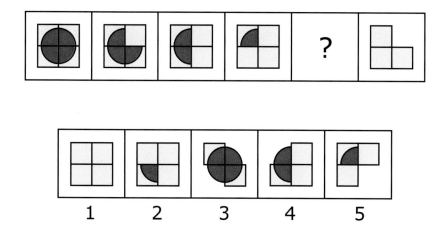

Answer on page 148

Question 57

What comes next in the pattern?

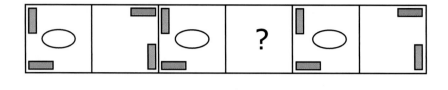

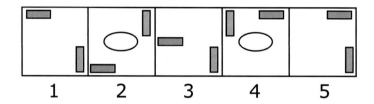

Question 58

What comes next in the pattern?

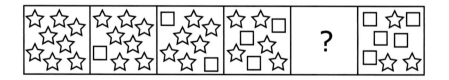

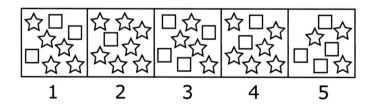

Question 59

What comes next in the pattern?

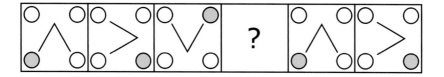

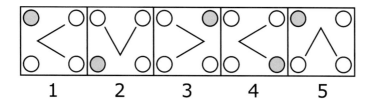

Question 60

What comes next in the pattern?

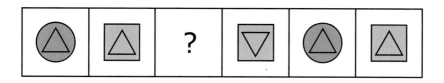

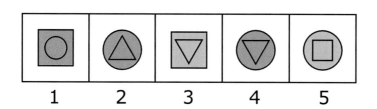

Figure Weights

Figure Weight is a new subtest of the WISC-V.
There are 20 questions from this subtest in this
practice book. 10 of them have one scale and the other
10 have two. Working within a time limit, the child
examines one or two scales balanced by weights and
a scale with missing weights, and then selects the
weights that keep the scale balanced from the
answer options.
Success!

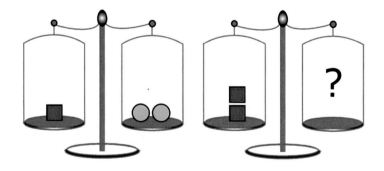

Question 61

Which of the figures below can balance the scale?

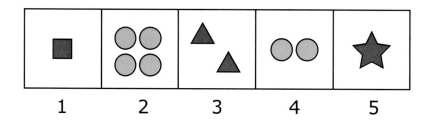

Question 62

Which of the figures below can balance the scale?

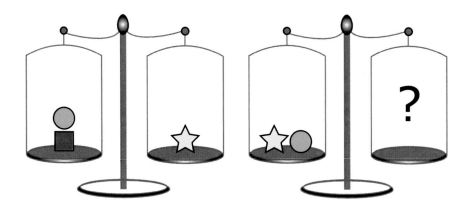

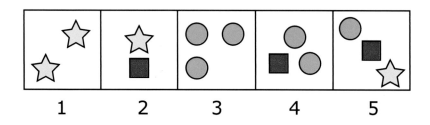

Question 63

Which of the figures below can balance the scale?

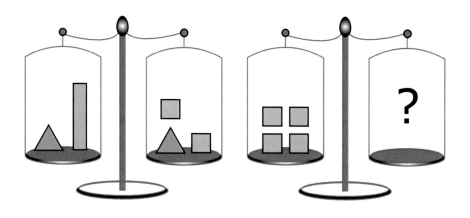

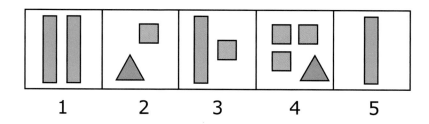

Question 64

Which of the figures below can balance the scale?

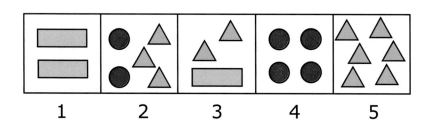

Question 65

Which of the figures below can balance the scale?

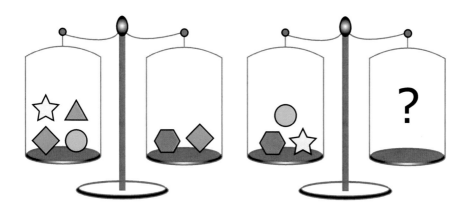

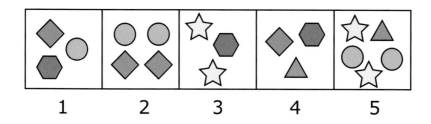

Question 66

Which of the figures below can balance the scale?

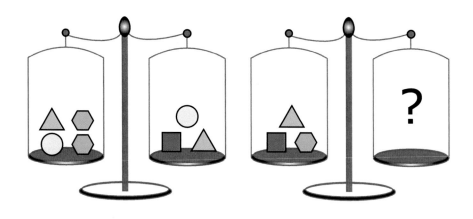

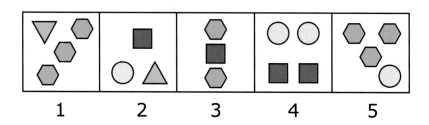

| 1 | 2 | 3 | 4 | 5 |

Question 67

Which of the figures below can balance the scale?

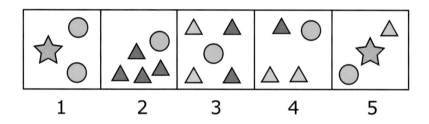

Question 68

Which of the figures below can balance the scale?

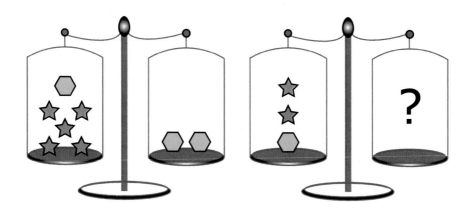

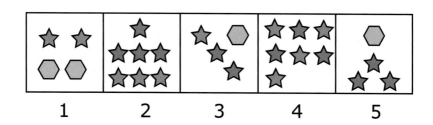

Question 69

Which of the figures below can balance the scale?

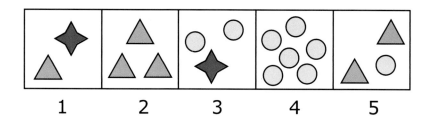

Question 70

Which of the figures below can balance the scale?

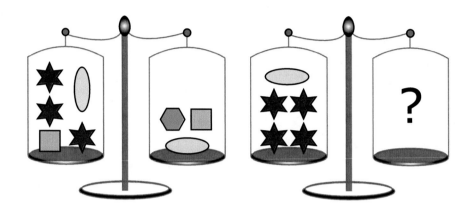

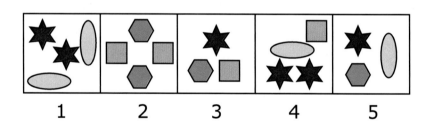

1	2	3	4	5

Question 71

Which of the figures below can balance the scale?

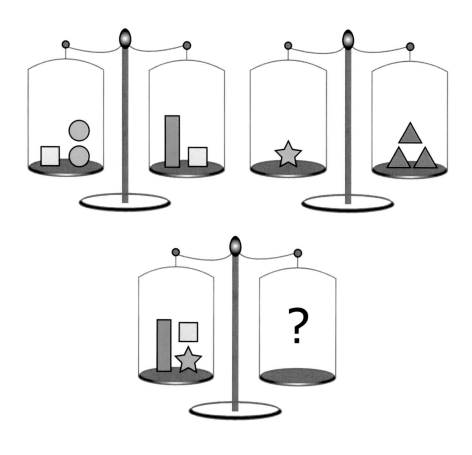

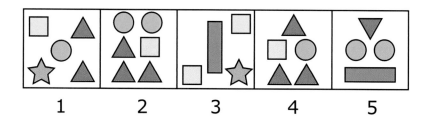

1 2 3 4 5

Question 72

Which of the figures below can balance the scale?

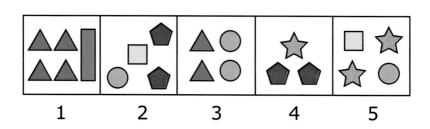

Answer on page 149

Question 73

Which of the figures below can balance the scale?

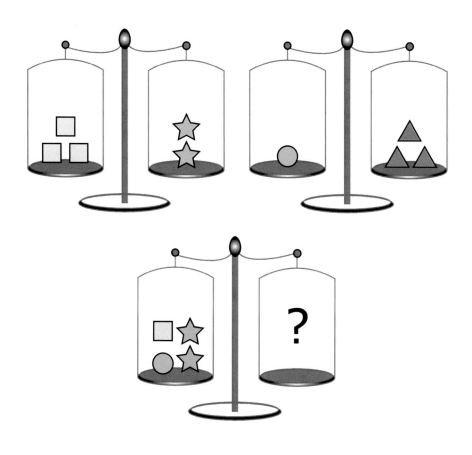

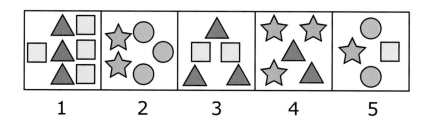

Question 74

Which of the figures below can balance the scale?

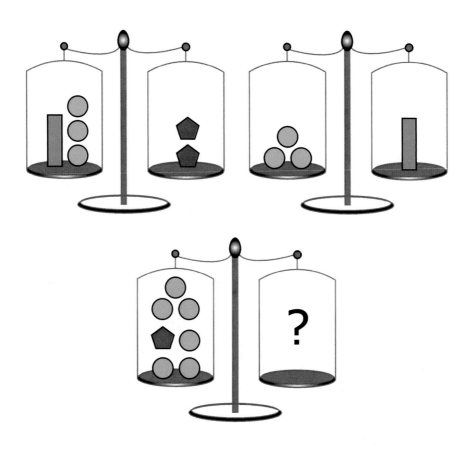

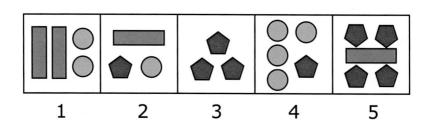

Question 75

Which of the figures below can balance the scale?

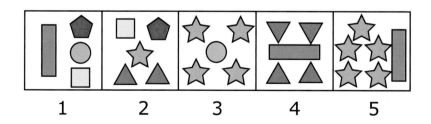

1   2   3   4   5

Question 76

Which of the figures below can balance the scale?

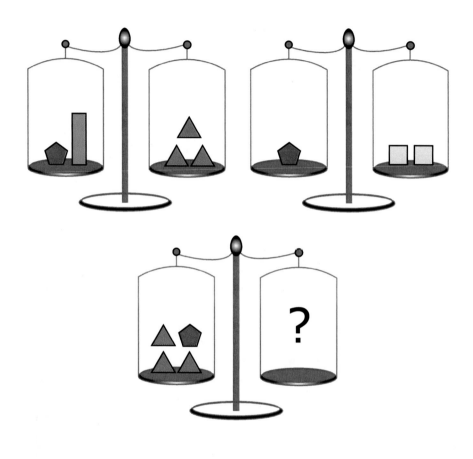

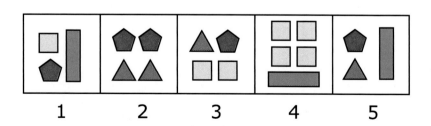

Question 77

Which of the figures below can balance the scale?

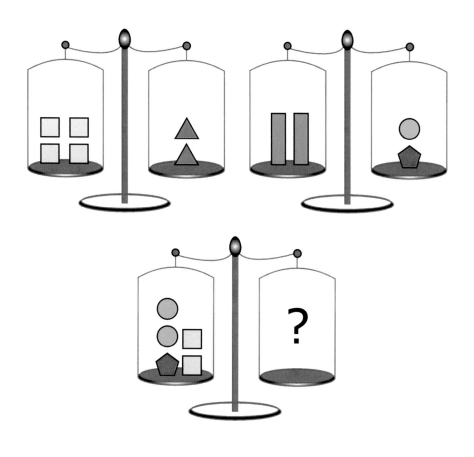

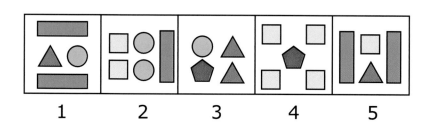

Question 78

Which of the figures below can balance the scale?

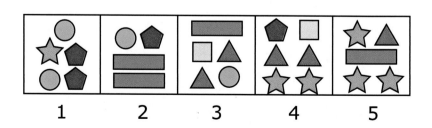

Question 79

Which of the figures below can balance the scale?

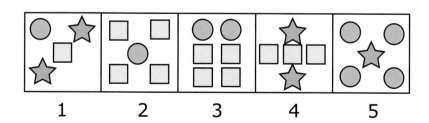

Question 80

Which of the figures below can balance the scale?

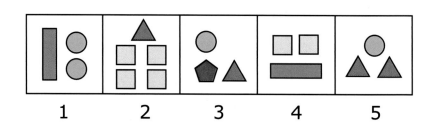

Coding

Codding is a timed Processing Speed subtest. There are 20 questions from this subtest in this practice book. 10 of them have five codes, and 10 of them have nine codes. Working within a time limit, the child uses a key to copy symbols that correspond to simple geometric shapes or letters. The light gray squares indicate an example of how the codes should be written.

Success!

Key

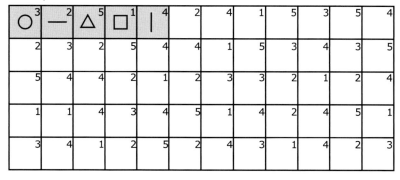

Sample

Question 81

Which symbol corresponds to each number in the worksheet provided ?

Key

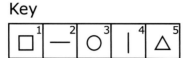

	1		2		3		4		5
□		—		○					△

Sample

○³	—²	△⁵	□¹	|⁴	2	4	1	5	3	5	4
2	3	2	5	4	4	1	5	3	4	3	5
5	4	4	2	1	2	3	3	2	1	2	4
1	1	4	3	4	5	1	4	2	4	5	1
3	4	1	2	5	2	4	3	1	4	2	3

Question 82

Which symbol corresponds to each number in the worksheet provided ?

Key

	1		2		3		4		5
=		×		>		∪			||

Sample

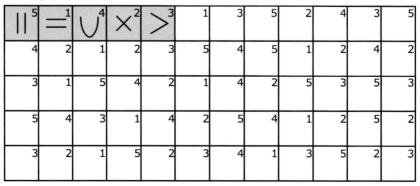

||⁵	=¹	∪⁴	×²	>³	1	3	5	2	4	3	5
4	2	1	2	3	5	4	5	1	2	4	2
3	1	5	4	2	1	4	2	5	3	5	3
5	4	3	1	4	2	5	4	1	2	5	2
3	2	1	5	2	3	4	1	3	5	2	3

Question 83

Which symbol corresponds to each number in the worksheet provided ?

Key

$<$ (1), $\bigcirc$ (2), $/$ (3), $\llcorner$ (4), $\vee$ (5)

Sample

$<$ ¹	$\vee$ ⁵	$\llcorner$ ⁴	$/$ ³	$\bigcirc$ ²	5	3	4	2	2	4	1
3	2	1	5	5	2	4	2	1	5	5	3
4	3	5	3	1	1	5	3	4	1	3	5
2	1	1	2	5	2	4	5	3	4	1	4
5	4	3	1	2	4	5	3	1	2	4	1

Question 84

Which symbol corresponds to each number in the worksheet provided ?

Key

$\wedge$ (1), $\ulcorner$ (2), $\square$ (3), $=$ (4), $\times$ (5)

Sample

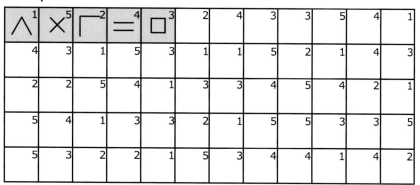

$\wedge$ ¹	$\times$ ⁵	$\ulcorner$ ²	$=$ ⁴	$\square$ ³	2	4	3	3	5	4	1
4	3	1	5	3	1	1	5	2	1	4	3
2	2	5	4	1	3	3	4	5	4	2	1
5	4	1	3	3	2	1	5	5	3	3	5
5	3	2	2	1	5	3	4	4	1	4	2

Question 85

Which symbol corresponds to each number in the worksheet provided ?

Key

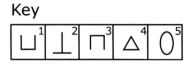

Sample

△⁴	⊓³	○⁵	⊔¹	⊥²	2	4	3	5	1	1	4
2	5	1	4	3	5	1	1	4	2	4	3
1	3	3	2	1	4	2	4	5	3	3	2
5	2	5	5	4	1	4	3	2	5	1	1
4	5	2	2	5	3	1	2	5	1	4	4

Question 86

Which symbol corresponds to each number in the worksheet provided ?

Key

Sample

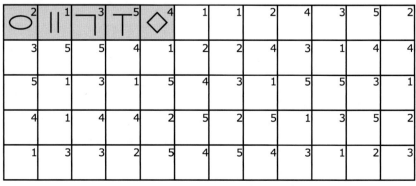

○²	‖¹	⊤³	T⁵	◇⁴	1	1	2	4	3	5	2
3	5	5	4	1	2	2	4	3	1	4	4
5	1	3	1	5	4	3	1	5	5	3	1
4	1	4	4	2	5	2	5	1	3	5	2
1	3	3	2	5	4	5	4	3	1	2	3

Question 87

Which symbol corresponds to each number in the worksheet provided ?

Key

Sample

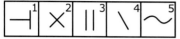

5	2	4	1	3	2	4	3	1	5	5	2
4	1	3	2	4	5	2	2	3	1	4	4
2	5	2	3	1	4	4	5	2	3	5	1
4	5	5	1	2	3	4	3	1	2	1	1
5	4	1	3	3	2	5	2	5	1	2	3

Question 88

Which symbol corresponds to each number in the worksheet provided ?

Key

$+^1 \quad <^2 \quad \div^3 \quad Z^4 \quad >^5$

Sample

2	1	4	3	5	3	2	4	1	5	5	4
3	2	1	4	2	1	2	5	4	3	3	2
5	1	3	2	4	5	1	2	5	1	4	4
4	5	4	5	1	3	2	3	1	5	3	1
1	4	2	3	2	2	4	5	3	2	4	5

Question 89

Which symbol corresponds to each number in the worksheet provided ?

Key

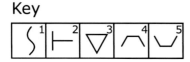

Sample

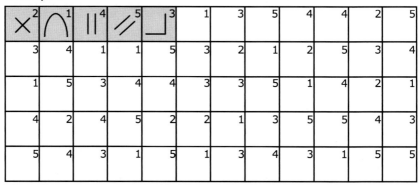

4	1	3	5	2	2	4	1	5	3	2	2
5	4	1	4	1	1	3	2	5	5	1	4
3	2	2	3	5	2	4	2	4	1	1	5
1	4	1	5	3	5	2	2	3	5	2	4
2	1	3	4	5	2	4	3	1	4	4	1

Question 90

Which symbol corresponds to each number in the worksheet provided ?

Key

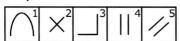

Sample

2	1	4	5	3	1	3	5	4	4	2	5
3	4	1	1	5	3	2	1	2	5	3	4
1	5	3	4	4	3	3	5	1	4	2	1
4	2	4	5	2	2	1	3	5	5	4	3
5	4	3	1	5	1	3	4	3	1	5	5

Question 91

Which symbol corresponds to each number in the worksheet provided ?

Key

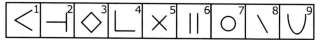

Sample

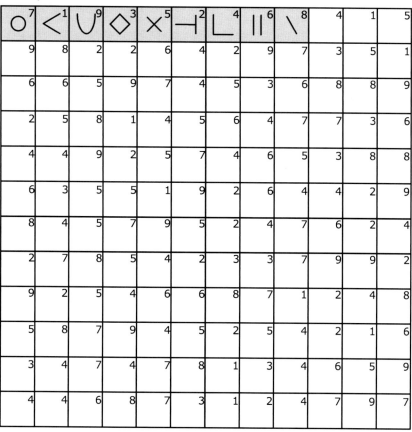

O	<	U	◇	×	⊣	L	||	\	4	1	5
9	8	2	2	6	4	2	9	7	3	5	1
6	6	5	9	7	4	5	3	6	8	8	9
2	5	8	1	4	5	6	4	7	7	3	6
4	4	9	2	5	7	4	6	5	3	8	8
6	3	5	5	1	9	2	6	4	4	2	9
8	4	5	7	9	5	2	4	7	6	2	4
2	7	8	5	4	2	3	3	7	9	9	2
9	2	5	4	6	6	8	7	1	2	4	8
5	8	7	9	4	5	2	5	4	2	1	6
3	4	7	4	7	8	1	3	4	6	5	9
4	4	6	8	7	3	1	2	4	7	9	7

Question 92

Which symbol corresponds to each number in the worksheet provided ?

Key

Sample

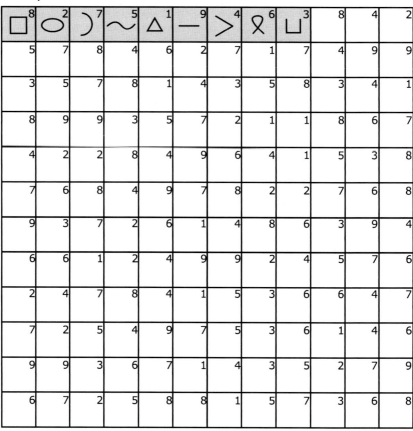

8	2	7	5	1	9	4	6	3	8	4	2
5	7	8	4	6	2	7	1	7	4	9	9
3	5	7	8	1	4	3	5	8	3	4	1
8	9	9	3	5	7	2	1	1	8	6	7
4	2	2	8	4	9	6	4	1	5	3	8
7	6	8	4	9	7	8	2	2	7	6	8
9	3	7	2	6	1	4	8	6	3	9	4
6	6	1	2	4	9	9	2	4	5	7	6
2	4	7	8	4	1	5	3	6	6	4	7
7	2	5	4	9	7	5	3	6	1	4	6
9	9	3	6	7	1	4	3	5	2	7	9
6	7	2	5	8	8	1	5	7	3	6	8

Answer on page 157

Question 93

Which symbol corresponds to each number in the worksheet provided ?

Key

$\triangledown$¹	✱²	V³	→⁴	○⁵	Z⁶	+⁷	>⁸	◊⁹

Sample

V³	▽¹	+⁷	→⁴	Z⁶	◊⁹	○⁵	✱²	>⁸	4	8	7
9	6	2	8	1	7	5	3	4	5	7	9
7	2	5	1	1	6	4	9	2	1	5	8
2	1	8	2	4	7	3	9	4	4	1	3
6	6	3	9	7	2	5	7	6	3	3	4
8	6	4	8	8	6	1	3	7	8	1	9
5	1	7	3	2	4	9	9	3	5	1	4
4	6	2	1	8	7	5	3	1	4	6	9
5	4	8	2	1	6	7	2	8	9	1	4
6	2	7	8	1	4	3	7	5	1	1	6
2	2	5	4	6	9	9	2	7	3	8	4
7	6	1	8	3	7	9	8	4	6	5	1

Question 94

Which symbol corresponds to each number in the worksheet provided ?

Key

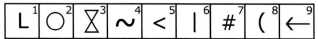

Sample

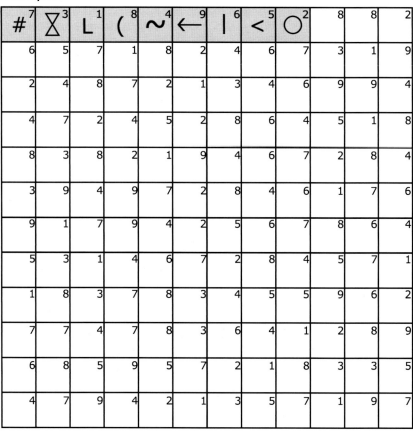

#⁷	⧖³	L¹	(⁸	~⁴	←⁹	|⁶	<⁵	O²	8	8	2
6	5	7	1	8	2	4	6	7	3	1	9
2	4	8	7	2	1	3	4	6	9	9	4
4	7	2	4	5	2	8	6	4	5	1	8
8	3	8	2	1	9	4	6	7	2	8	4
3	9	4	9	7	2	8	4	6	1	7	6
9	1	7	9	4	2	5	6	7	8	6	4
5	3	1	4	6	7	2	8	4	5	7	1
1	8	3	7	8	3	4	5	5	9	6	2
7	7	4	7	8	3	6	4	1	2	8	9
6	8	5	9	5	7	2	1	8	3	3	5
4	7	9	4	2	1	3	5	7	1	9	7

Question 95

Which symbol corresponds to each number in the worksheet provided ?

Key

⊗ 1	⌐ 2	/ 3	Y 4	□ 5	⊔ 6	} 7	∧ 8	# 9

Sample

} 7	⊗ 1	□ 5	# 9	/ 3	Y 4	∧ 8	⊔ 6	⌐ 2	8	4	7
6	8	7	3	6	1	1	7	6	3	3	9
2	4	2	6	7	9	4	2	3	7	9	6
9	7	5	5	9	1	2	2	7	3	8	1
4	4	8	1	6	2	7	7	8	3	1	9
8	6	5	2	7	1	2	2	7	6	4	7
5	8	3	9	9	4	7	6	3	3	7	5
1	1	8	4	6	7	2	8	3	9	9	4
4	7	5	3	9	2	4	6	4	7	6	1
7	6	8	2	2	7	4	1	8	2	7	7
6	8	2	1	7	6	8	4	1	8	3	6
9	2	8	7	3	1	4	7	2	7	6	4

Question 96

Which symbol corresponds to each number in the worksheet provided ?

Key

$\downarrow$ 1	Ǝ 2	= 3	{ 4	H 5	S 6	▧ 7	+ 8	[] 9

Sample

{ 4	+ 8	Ǝ 2	S 6	↓ 1	= 3	H 5	[] 9	▧ 7	4	5	1
9	5	3	7	3	2	9	4	5	2	8	7
5	7	4	9	3	7	4	2	8	4	9	5
3	9	8	2	7	4	6	8	1	1	8	9
6	6	4	3	5	2	1	7	8	3	3	7
2	1	2	1	8	7	7	6	2	4	4	8
7	2	9	9	1	3	4	5	5	8	3	2
1	5	1	3	4	7	9	6	9	7	7	4
4	4	5	1	3	2	9	7	5	3	4	8
8	6	6	1	7	8	3	5	7	8	6	6
6	1	5	3	7	9	9	5	4	1	8	3
5	2	4	9	2	1	3	8	6	7	1	1

Question 97

Which symbol corresponds to each number in the worksheet provided ?

Key

⫫¹	x²	⊥³	Φ⁴	▷⁵	◡⁶	∏⁷	◠⁸	>⁹

Sample

▷⁵	⫫¹	◠⁸	⊥³	◡⁶	>⁹	Φ⁴	∏⁷	x²	6	4	4
9	3	2	7	5	8	1	1	7	5	1	9
2	4	6	8	7	5	3	1	9	4	5	8
6	3	1	4	5	9	9	7	2	5	4	8
8	1	7	3	7	8	4	1	7	9	3	7
3	6	1	8	2	7	6	2	4	3	8	5
7	7	3	1	7	3	8	1	2	7	2	6
2	5	9	4	2	1	5	3	1	4	8	1
4	8	2	9	9	7	4	6	3	5	4	7
1	6	7	7	1	3	5	9	4	1	7	4
8	2	5	3	9	7	4	4	3	6	1	1
5	7	9	7	5	3	1	8	6	4	2	2

Question 98

Which symbol corresponds to each number in the worksheet provided ?

Key

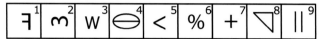

Sample

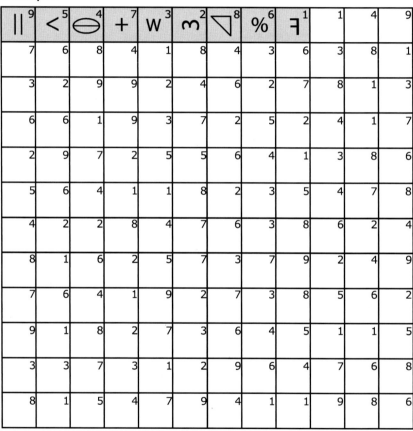

Question 99

Which symbol corresponds to each number in the worksheet provided ?

Key

L¹	)²	U³	#⁴	↗⁵	*⁶	⚠⁷	;⁸	S⁹

Sample

⚠⁷	L¹	*⁶	S⁹	#⁴	↗⁵	;⁸	U³	)²			
3	5	7	1	6	9	9	4	6	1	7	5
8	1	4	6	7	3	5	5	9	8	4	1
4	9	5	6	3	8	2	1	7	6	4	9
6	6	4	7	3	7	7	2	1	7	3	8
5	1	7	4	9	9	5	3	2	8	2	4
9	1	8	3	2	7	5	8	4	6	9	1
2	8	5	7	4	3	3	6	7	2	8	4
1	6	6	2	7	4	9	5	5	1	6	7
3	9	4	1	8	2	4	7	3	9	9	2
6	2	8	4	7	6	2	3	4	8	1	9
8	1	3	5	6	2	2	9	4	7	2	3

Question 100

Which symbol corresponds to each number in the worksheet provided ?

Key

Sample

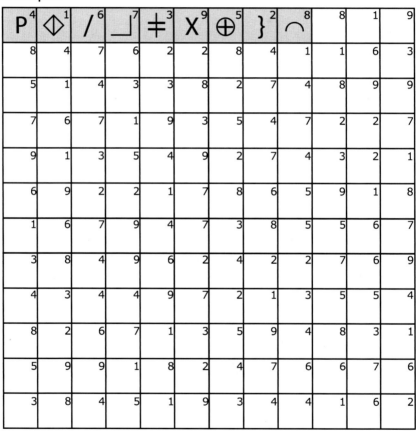

P⁴	◇¹	/⁶	⌐⁷	≠³	X⁹	⊕⁵	}²	⌒⁸	8	1	9
8	4	7	6	2	2	8	4	1	1	6	3
5	1	4	3	3	8	2	7	4	8	9	9
7	6	7	1	9	3	5	4	7	2	2	7
9	1	3	5	4	9	2	7	4	3	2	1
6	9	2	2	1	7	8	6	5	9	1	8
1	6	7	9	4	7	3	8	5	5	6	7
3	8	4	9	6	2	4	2	2	7	6	9
4	3	4	4	9	7	2	1	3	5	5	4
8	2	6	7	1	3	5	9	4	8	3	1
5	9	9	1	8	2	4	7	6	6	7	6
3	8	4	5	1	9	3	4	4	1	6	2

Symbol Search

Symbol Search is a timed Processing Speed subtest. There are 20 questions from this subtest in this practice book. In the first 10 questions, only one symbol is required, and in the other 10, two symbols are required. This subtest requires the child to determine whether a target symbol(s) appears among the symbols displayed in a search group.

Success!

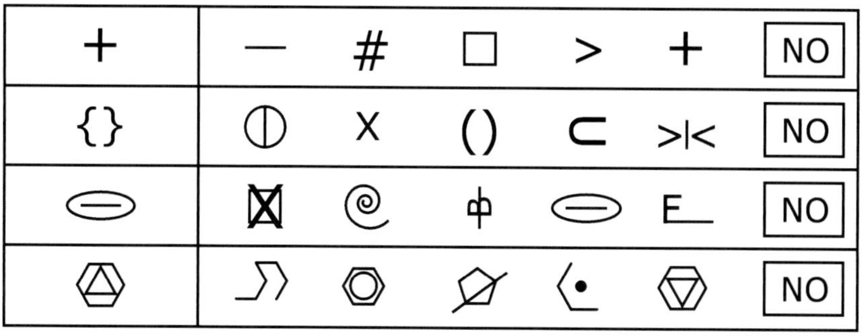

+	—	#	□	>	+	NO
{}	⦶	X	()	⊂	>|<	NO
⬭	�Xⵏ	@	ɸ	⬭	Ε_	NO
⬡	⟩⟩	◎	⬠	⟨•	⬡	NO

Question 101

*Check the symbols on the right to see if any of them
match the symbol on the left.*

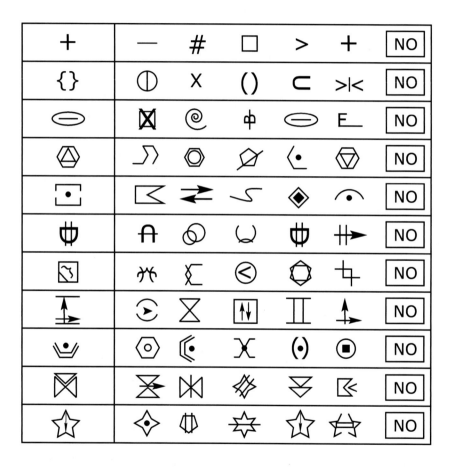

Answer on page 165

Question 102

Check the symbols on the right to see if any of them match the symbol on the left.

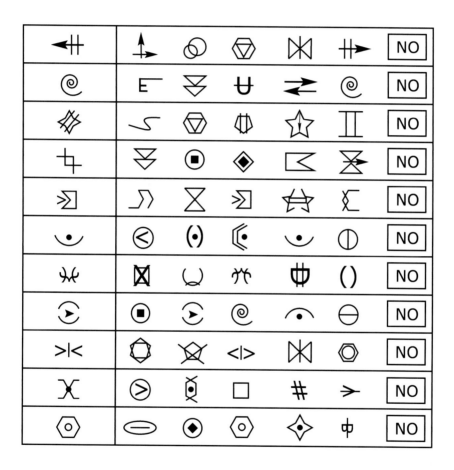

Question 103

*Check the symbols on the right to see if any of them
match the symbol on the left.*

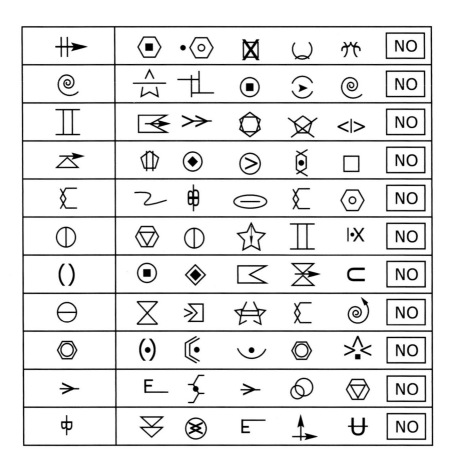

Answer on page 165

Question 104

Check the symbols on the right to see if any of them match the symbol on the left.

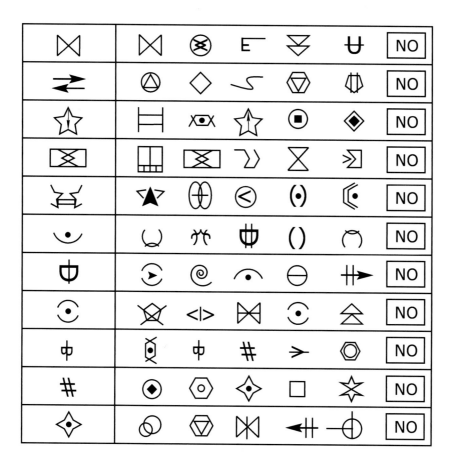

Question 105

Check the symbols on the right to see if any of them match the symbol on the left.

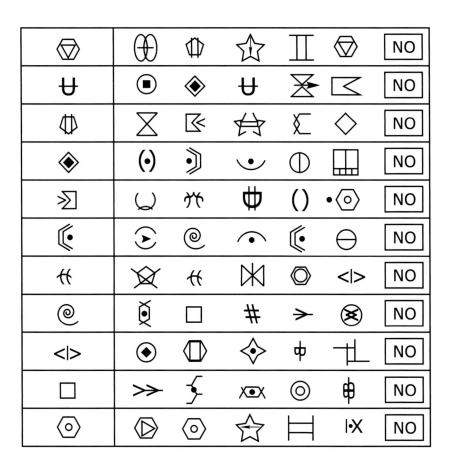

Question 106

Check the symbols on the right to see if any of them match the symbol on the left.

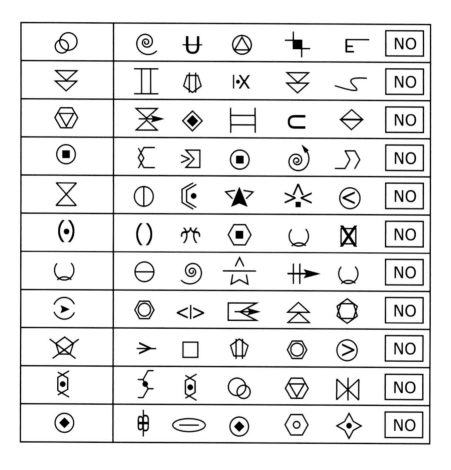

Question 107

Check the symbols on the right to see if any of them match the symbol on the left.

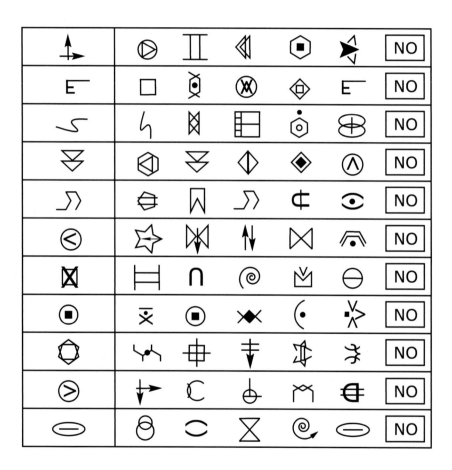

Question 108

Check the symbols on the right to see if any of them match the symbol on the left.

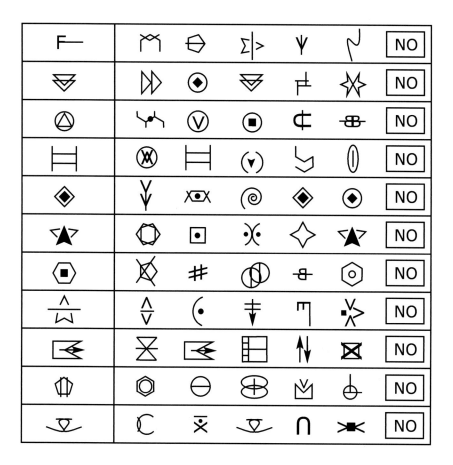

Question 109

*Check the symbols on the right to see if any of them
match the symbol on the left.*

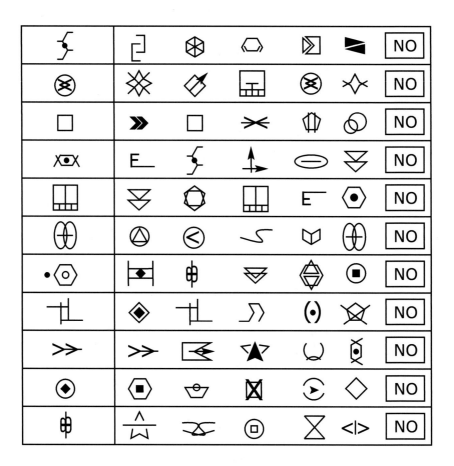

Question 110

Check the symbols on the right to see if any of them match the symbol on the left.

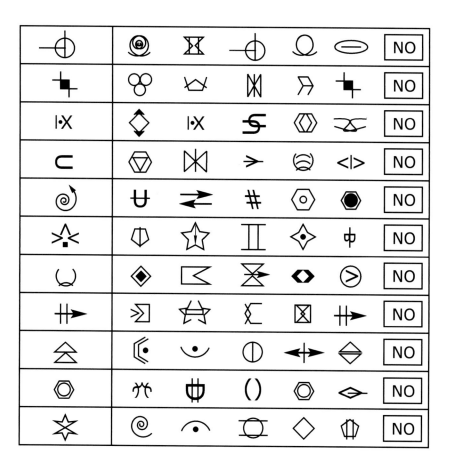

Question 111

*Check the symbols on the right to see if any of them
match the two symbols on the left.*

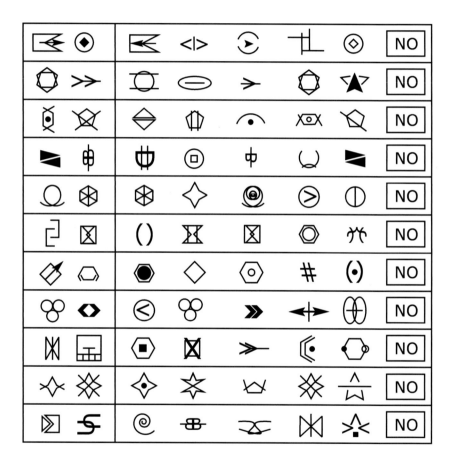

Question 112

Check the symbols on the right to see if any of them match the two symbols on the left.

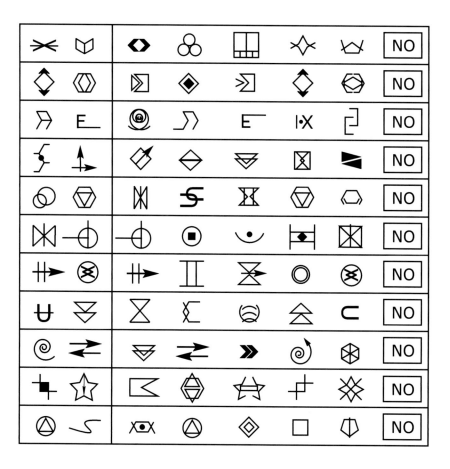

Question 113

Check the symbols on the right to see if any of them match the two symbols on the left.

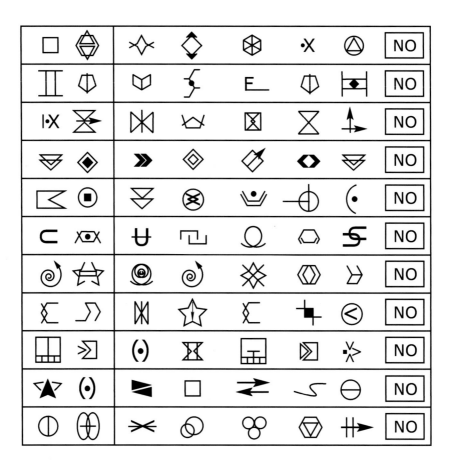

Question 114

Check the symbols on the right to see if any of them match the two symbols on the left.

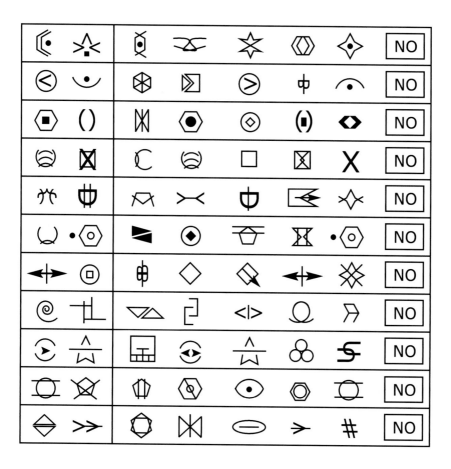

Question 115

*Check the symbols on the right to see if any of them
match the two symbols on the left.*

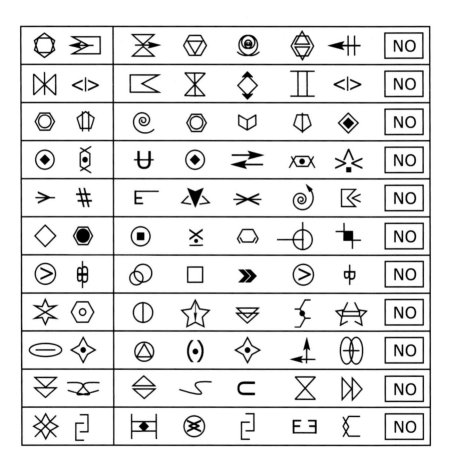

Question 116

Check the symbols on the right to see if any of them match the two symbols on the left.

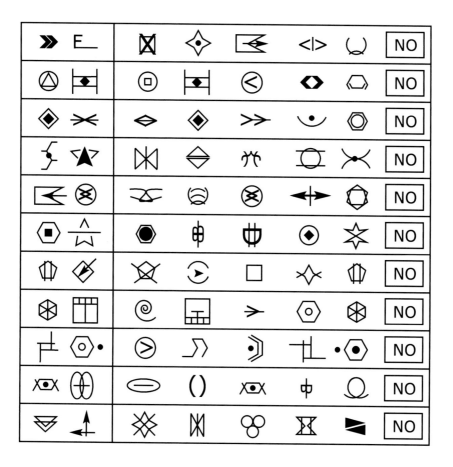

Question 117

Check the symbols on the right to see if any of them match the two symbols on the left.

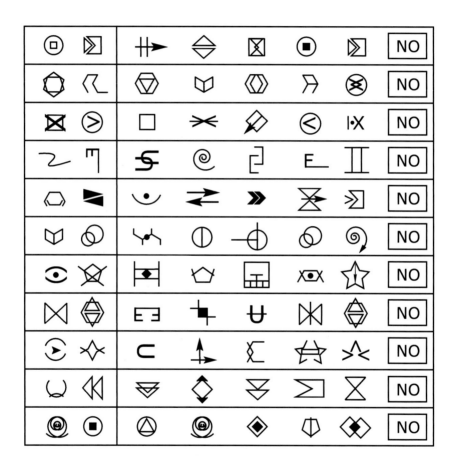

Question 118

Check the symbols on the right to see if any of them match the two symbols on the left.

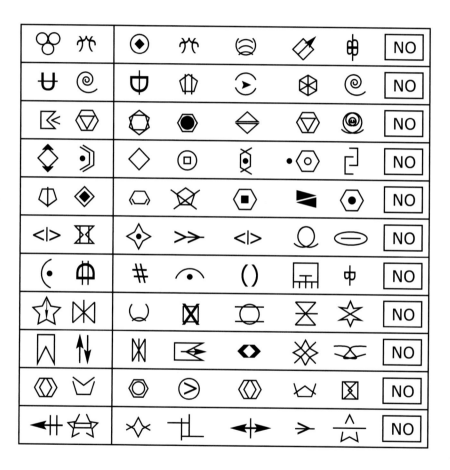

Question 119

Check the symbols on the right to see if any of them match the two symbols on the left.

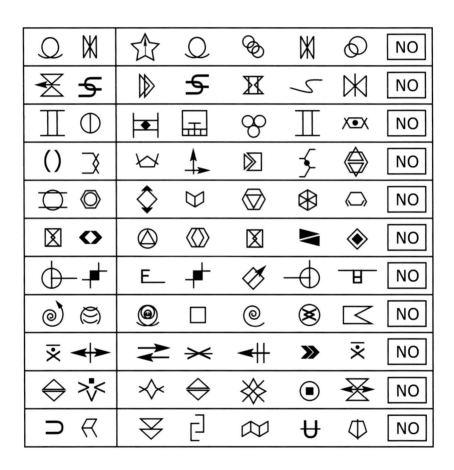

Question 120

Check the symbols on the right to see if any of them match the two symbols on the left.

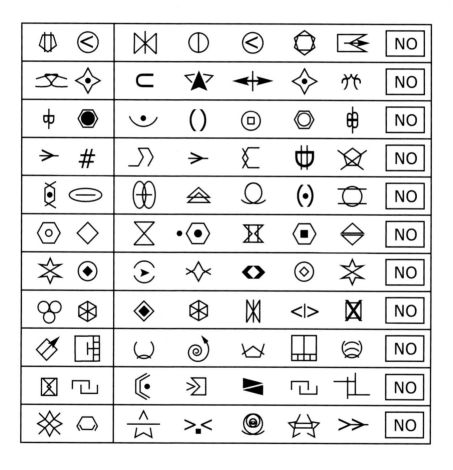

Cancellation

*Cancellation is a timed Processing Speed
subtest. There are 10 questions from this subtest
in this practice book. The child sees two arrangements
of shapes (one structured and one random). The
child's task is to identify all matches of the target
shapes and mark them.*
Success!

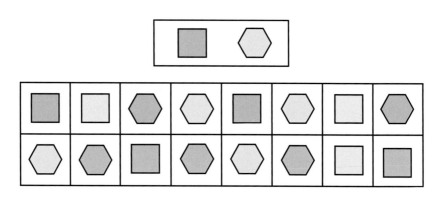

Question 121

Cross out each shape below that matches the example shapes

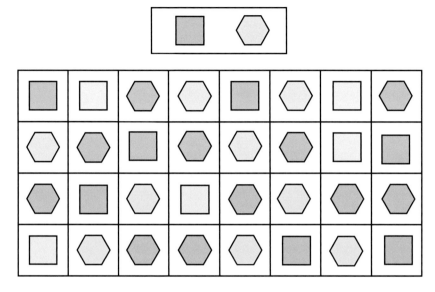

Question 122

Cross out each shape below that matches the example shapes

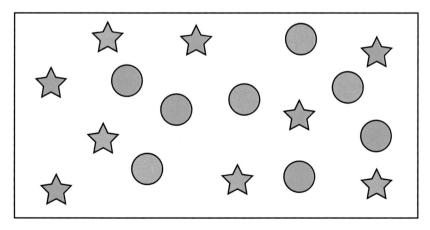

Question 123

Cross out each shape below that matches the example shapes

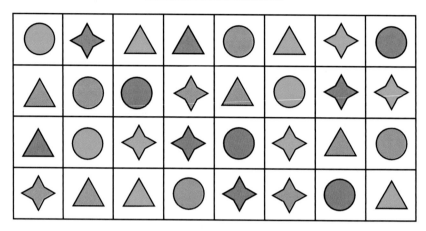

Question 124

Cross out each shape below that matches the example shapes

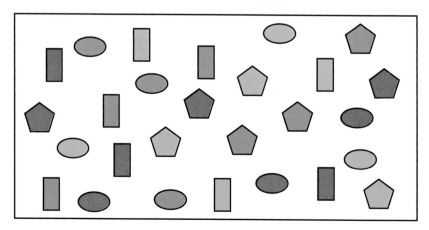

Question 125

Cross out each shape below that matches the example shapes

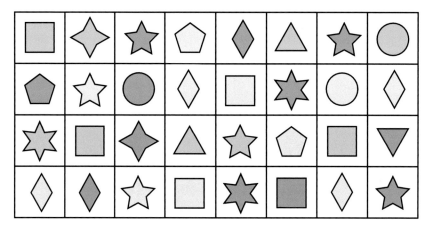

Question 126

Cross out each shape below that matches the example shapes

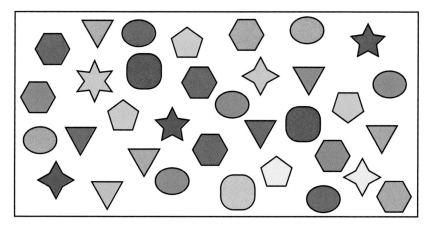

Question 127

Cross out each shape below that matches the example shapes

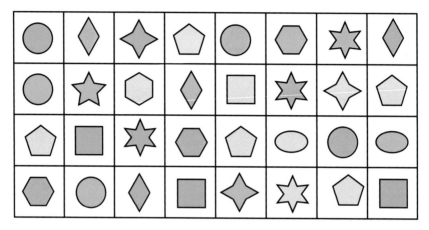

Question 128

Cross out each shape below that matches the example shapes

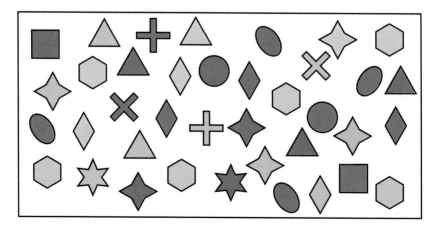

Question 129

*Cross out each shape below that matches the
example shapes*

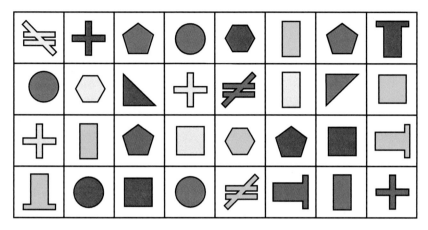

Question 130

*Cross out each shape below that matches the
example shapes*

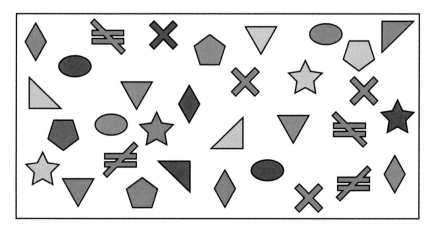

Block Design

(with 4 and 9 pieces)

The Block Design is a subtest of the Wechsler Intelligence Scale for Children/WISC®-V). This subtest is designed to assess visual-spatial, organizational, and nonverbal problem-solving abilities. It is a timed test, therefore fine motor abilities are also a factor. The child is shown similar blocks with solid red surfaces, solid white surfaces, and surfaces that are half red and half white. The test-taker is required to duplicate a pattern that is presented to them by the test-administrator, first as a physical model and then as a two-dimensional image, using an increasing number of these blocks.

Instructions about
how to make a paper cube

1. Download the free cube template: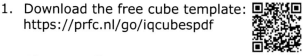
   https://prfc.nl/go/iqcubespdf

   Alternativelly, you can order our IQ Cubes
   from: https://prfc.nl/go/amzniqcubes

2. Print this page 9 times.
3. Cut alonge the outside edge.
Fold inward along the inside lines.
4. Apply glue to the designated locations.
5. Create a cube. Create 9 identical cubes by
repeating the process with the 9 copies.

Required tools:
 - Printer
 - Scissors
 - Glue

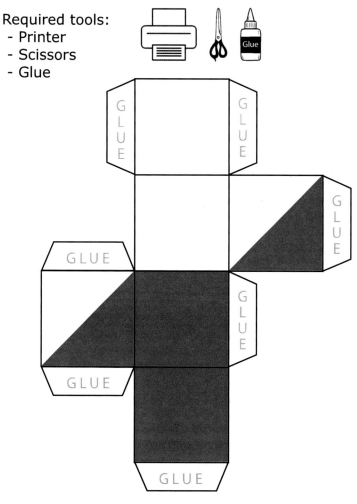

Block Design
(with 4 pieces)

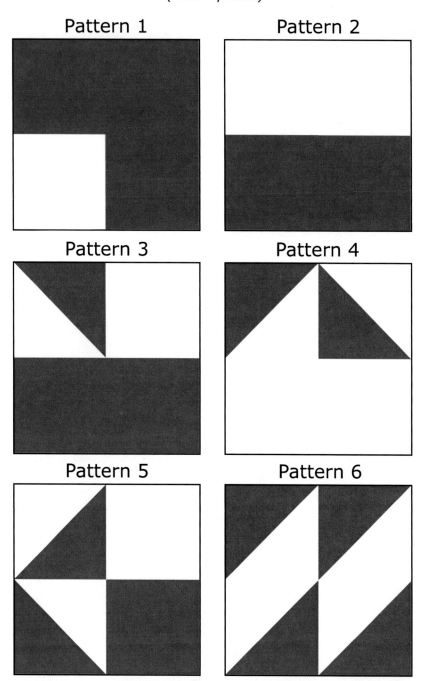

Block Design
(with 4 pieces)

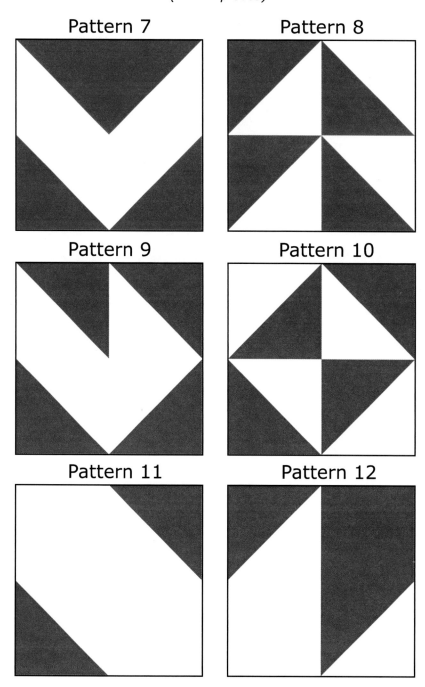

Pattern 7

Pattern 8

Pattern 9

Pattern 10

Pattern 11

Pattern 12

Block Design
(with 4 pieces)

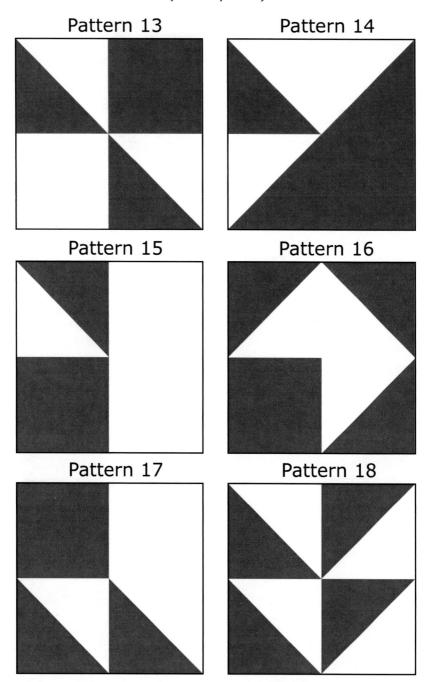

Pattern 13

Pattern 14

Pattern 15

Pattern 16

Pattern 17

Pattern 18

Block Design
(with 4 pieces)

Pattern 19

Pattern 20

Pattern 21

Pattern 22

Pattern 23

Pattern 24

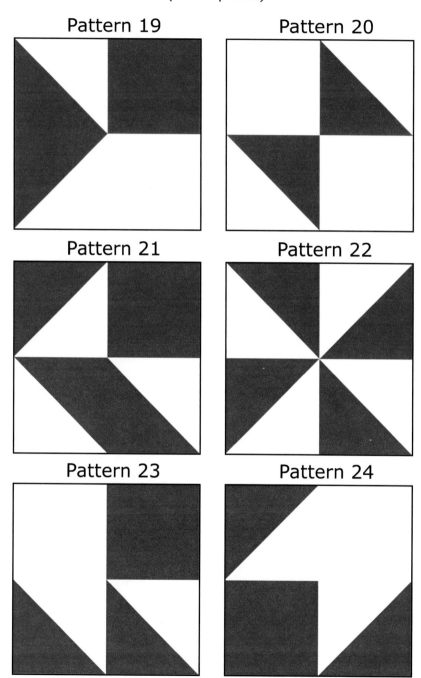

Block Design
(with 4 pieces)

Pattern 25

Pattern 26

Pattern 27

Pattern 28

Pattern 29

Pattern 30

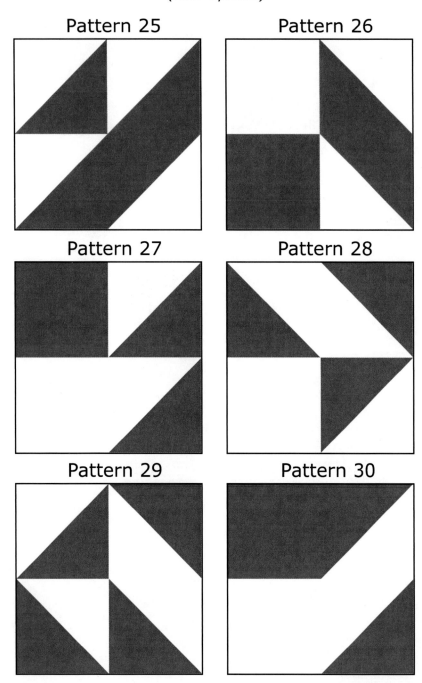

Block Design
(with 9 pieces)

Pattern 31

Pattern 32

Block Design
(with 9 pieces)

Pattern 33

Pattern 34

Block Design
(with 9 pieces)

Pattern 35

Pattern 36

Block Design
(with 9 pieces)

Pattern 37

Pattern 38

Block Design
(with 9 pieces)

Pattern 39

Pattern 40

Answer on page 182

Block Design
(with 9 pieces)

Pattern 41

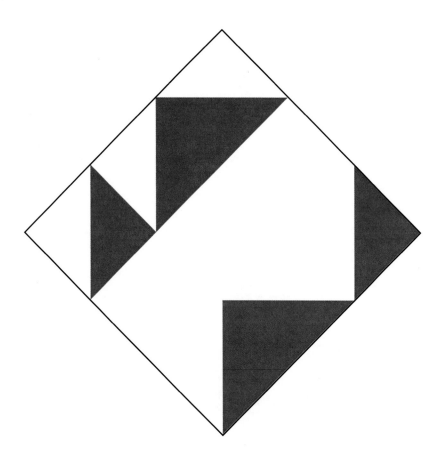

Block Design
(with 9 pieces)

Pattern 42

Block Design
(with 9 pieces)

Pattern 43

Answer on page 185

Block Design
(with 9 pieces)

Pattern 44

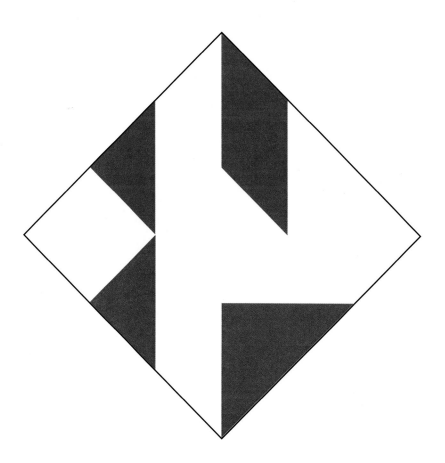

Block Design
(with 9 pieces)

Pattern 45

Block Design
(with 9 pieces)

Pattern 46

Answer on page 188

Block Design
(with 9 pieces)

Pattern 47

Answer on page 189

Block Design
(with 9 pieces)

Pattern 48

Block Design
(with 9 pieces)

Pattern 49

Answer on page 191

Block Design
(with 9 pieces)

Pattern 50

ANSWERS

Visual Puzzles
Answers

1. A	5. D	9. B	13. B	17. D
2. B	6. A	10. C	14. C	18. C
3. C	7. C	11. D	15. D	19. B
4. B	8. C	12. C	16. A	20. A

Matrix Reasoning
Answers

21. 2	29. 6	37. 1	45. 4	53. 5
22. 4	30. 3	38. 5	46. 5	54. 2
23. 6	31. 4	39. 5	47. 3	55. 4
24. 4	32. 2	40. 1	48. 5	56. 1
25. 3	33. 1	41. 4	49. 2	57. 5
26. 5	34. 2	42. 1	50. 1	58. 3
27. 1	35. 3	43. 3	51. 4	59. 1
28. 5	36. 5	44. 2	52. 3	60. 4

Figure Weights
Answers

61. 2	65. 5	69. 4	73. 1	77. 1
62. 4	66. 1	70. 5	74. 3	78. 4
63. 1	67. 3	71. 2	75. 5	79. 3
64. 2	68. 2	72. 4	76. 4	80. 5

Coding
Answers

Key

□¹	—²	○³	|⁴	△⁵

Question 81

Sample

○³	—²	△⁵	□¹	|⁴	—²	|⁴	□¹	△⁵	○³	△⁵	|⁴
—²	○³	—²	△⁵	|⁴	|⁴	□¹	△⁵	○³	|⁴	○³	△⁵
△⁵	|⁴	|⁴	—²	□¹	—²	○³	○³	—²	□¹	—²	|⁴
□¹	□¹	|⁴	○³	|⁴	△⁵	□¹	|⁴	—²	|⁴	△⁵	□¹
○³	|⁴	□¹	—²	△⁵	—²	|⁴	○³	□¹	|⁴	—²	○³

Key

=¹	×²	>³	∪⁴	‖⁵

Question 82

Sample

‖⁵	=¹	∪⁴	×²	>³	=¹	>³	‖⁵	×²	∪⁴	>³	‖⁵
∪⁴	×²	=¹	×²	>³	‖⁵	∪⁴	‖⁵	=¹	×²	∪⁴	×²
>³	=¹	‖⁵	∪⁴	×²	=¹	∪⁴	×²	‖⁵	>³	‖⁵	>³
‖⁵	∪⁴	>³	=¹	∪⁴	×²	‖⁵	∪⁴	=¹	×²	‖⁵	×²
>³	×²	=¹	‖⁵	×²	>³	∪⁴	=¹	>³	‖⁵	×²	>³

Coding
Answers

Key

Question 83

Sample

Key

Question 84

Sample

Coding
Answers

Key

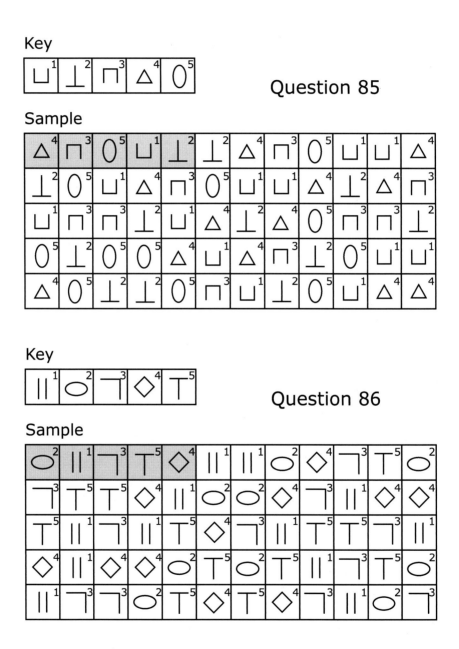

Question 85

Sample

Key

Question 86

Sample

152

Coding
Answers

Key

Question 87

Sample

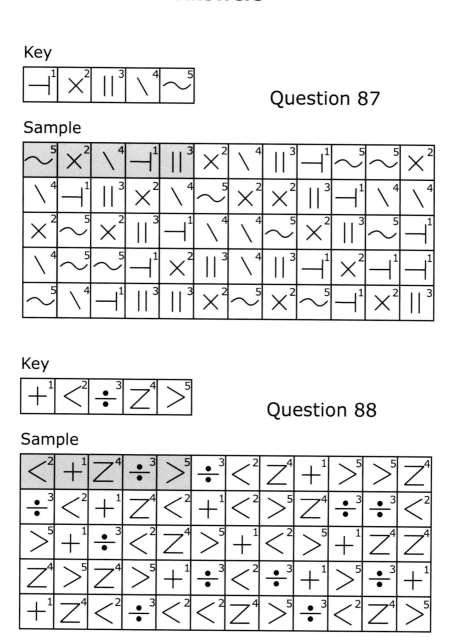

Key

Question 88

Sample

Coding
Answers

Key

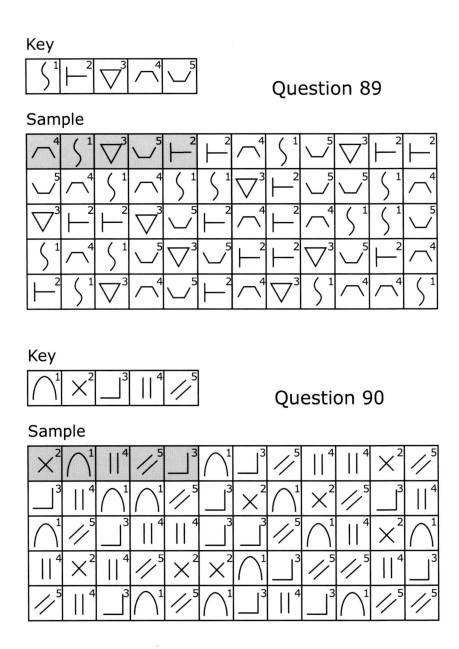

Question 89

Sample

Key

Question 90

Sample

Coding
Answers

Question 91

Key

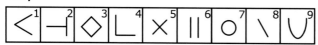

Sample

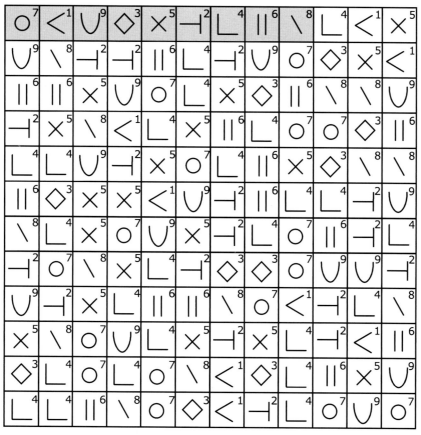

Coding
Answers

Question 92

Key

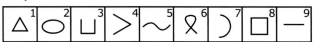

Sample

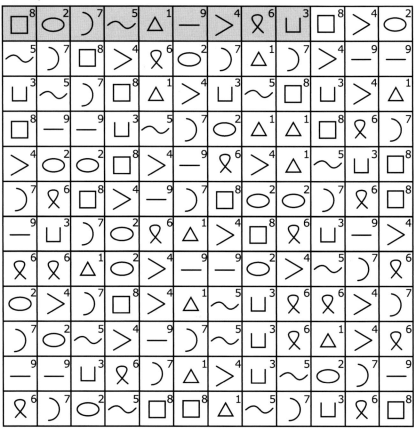

Coding
Answers

Question 93

Key

▽¹	*²	V³	→⁴	○⁵	Z⁶	+⁷	>⁸	◊⁹

Sample ▽ * V → ○ Z + > ◊

V³	▽¹	+⁷	→⁴	Z⁶	◊⁹	○⁵	*²	>⁸	→⁴	>⁸	+⁷
◊⁹	Z⁶	*²	>⁸	▽¹	+⁷	○⁵	V³	→⁴	○⁵	+⁷	◊⁹
+⁷	*²	○⁵	▽¹	▽¹	Z⁶	→⁴	◊⁹	*²	▽¹	○⁵	>⁸
*²	▽¹	>⁸	*²	→⁴	+⁷	V³	◊⁹	→⁴	→⁴	▽¹	V³
Z⁶	Z⁶	V³	◊⁹	+⁷	*²	○⁵	+⁷	Z⁶	V³	V³	→⁴
>⁸	Z⁶	→⁴	>⁸	>⁸	Z⁶	▽¹	V³	+⁷	>⁸	▽¹	◊⁹
○⁵	▽¹	+⁷	V³	*²	→⁴	◊⁹	◊⁹	V³	○⁵	▽¹	→⁴
→⁴	Z⁶	*²	▽¹	>⁸	+⁷	○⁵	V³	▽¹	→⁴	Z⁶	◊⁹
○⁵	→⁴	>⁸	*²	▽¹	Z⁶	+⁷	*²	>⁸	◊⁹	▽¹	→⁴
Z⁶	*²	+⁷	>⁸	▽¹	→⁴	V³	+⁷	○⁵	▽¹	▽¹	Z⁶
*²	*²	○⁵	→⁴	Z⁶	◊⁹	◊⁹	*²	+⁷	V³	>⁸	→⁴
+⁷	Z⁶	▽¹	>⁸	V³	+⁷	◊⁹	>⁸	→⁴	Z⁶	○⁵	▽¹

157

Coding
Answers

Question 94

Key

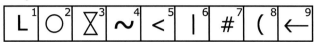

Sample

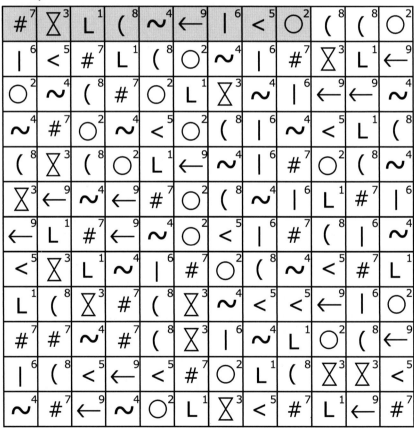

Coding
Answers

Question 95

Key

Sample

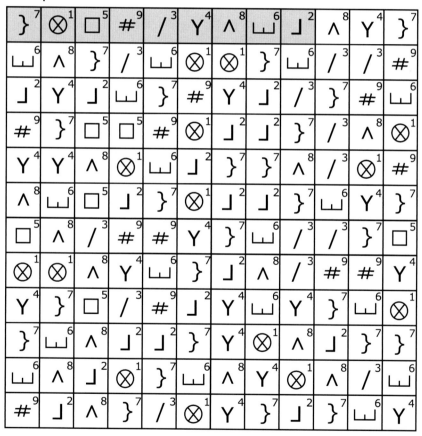

Coding
Answers

Question 96

Key

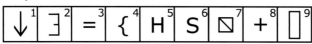

Sample

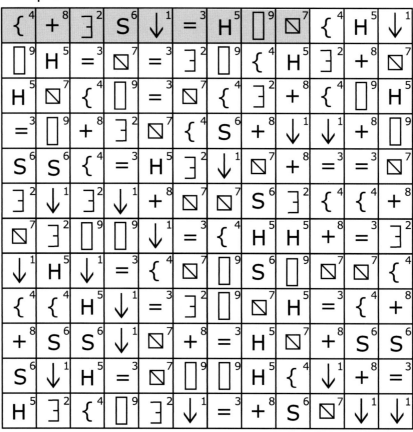

Coding
Answers

Question 97

Key

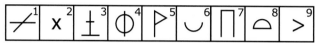

Sample

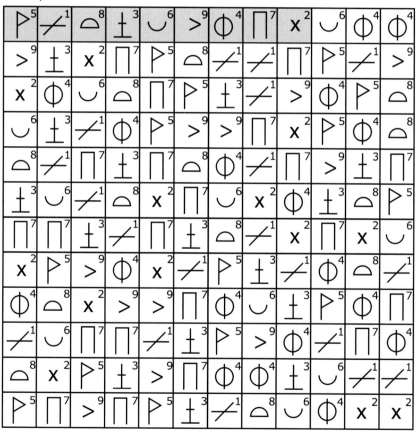

Coding
Answers

Question 98

Key

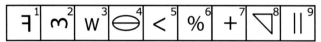

Sample

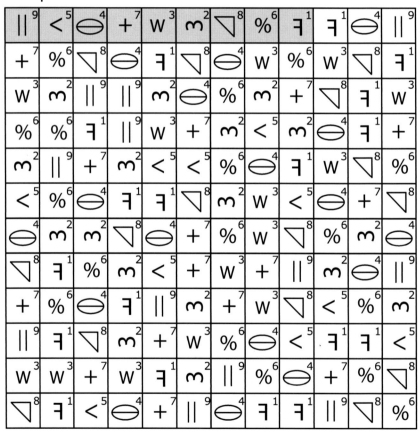

Coding
Answers

Question 99

Key

Sample

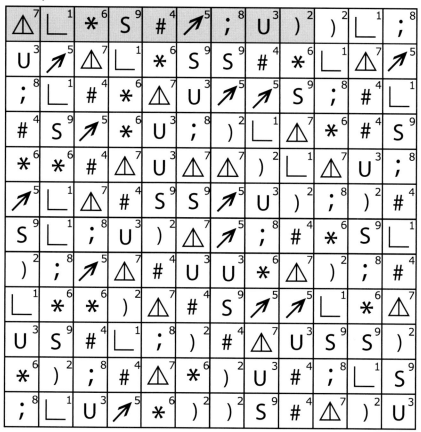

Coding
Answers

Question 100

Key

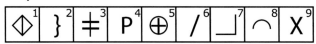

Sample

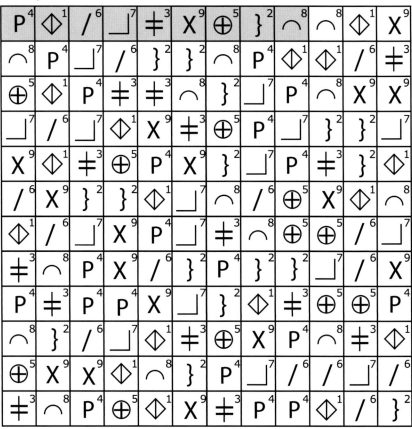

Symbol Search
Answers

Question 101

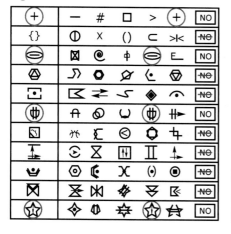

Question 102

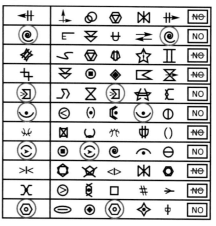

Question 103

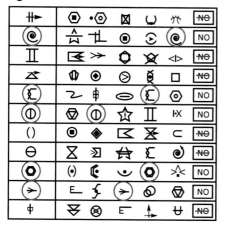

Question 104

Symbol Search
Answers

Question 105

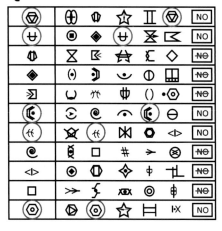

Question 106

Question 107

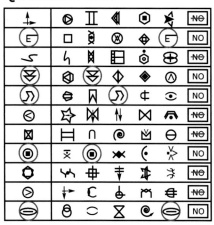

Question 108

Symbol Search
Answers

Question 109

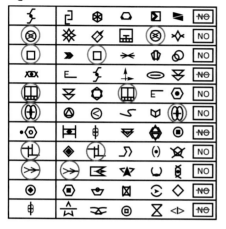

Question 110

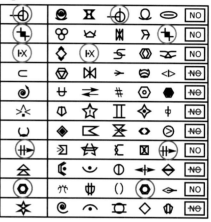

Question 111

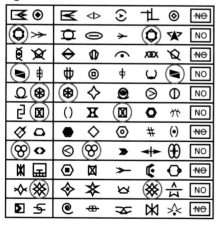

Question 112

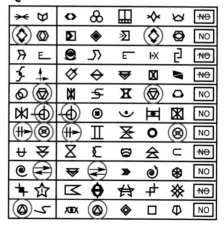

Symbol Search
Answers

Question 113

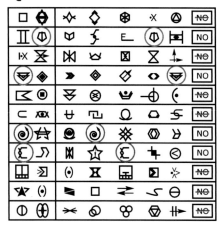

Question 114

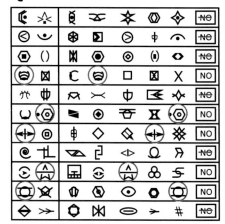

Question 115

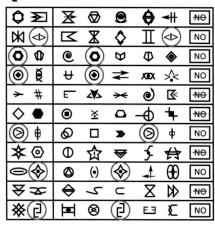

Question 116

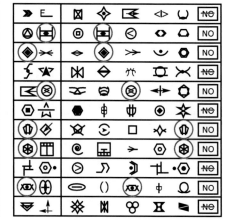

Symbol Search
Answers

Question 117

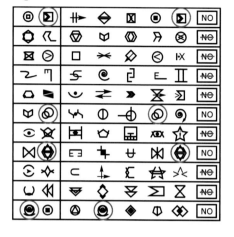

Question 118

Question 119

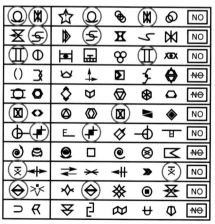

Question 120

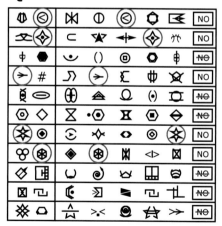

Cancellation
Answers

Question 121

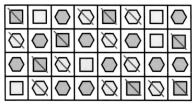

Question 122

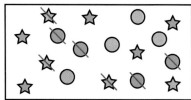

Question 123

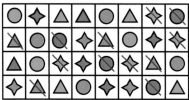

Question 124

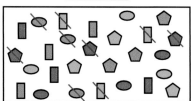

Question 125

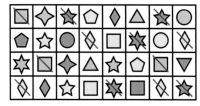

Question 126

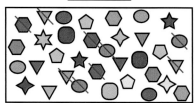

Cancellation
Answers

Question 127

Question 128

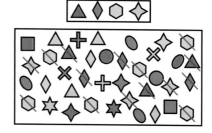

Question 129

Question 130

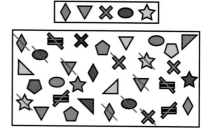

Block Design
Answers

Pattern 1

Pattern 2

Pattern 3

Pattern 4

Pattern 5

Pattern 6

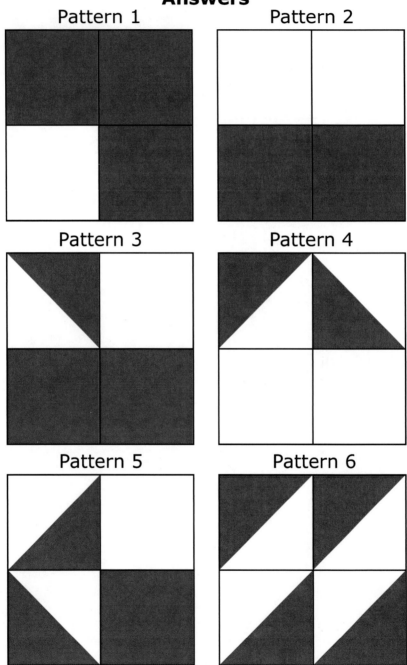

Block Design
Answers

Pattern 7

Pattern 8

Pattern 9

Pattern 10

Pattern 11

Pattern 12

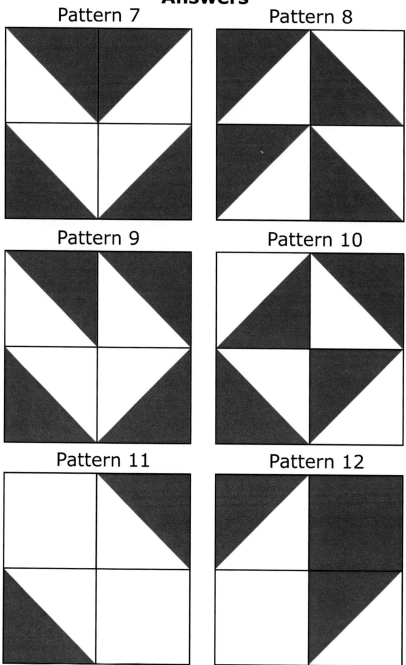

Block Design
Answers

Pattern 13

Pattern 14

Pattern 15

Pattern 16

Pattern 17

Pattern 18

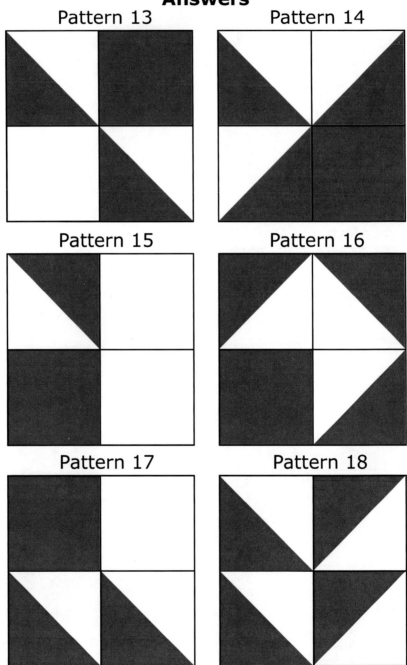

Block Design
Answers

Pattern 19

Pattern 20

Pattern 21

Pattern 22

Pattern 23

Pattern 24

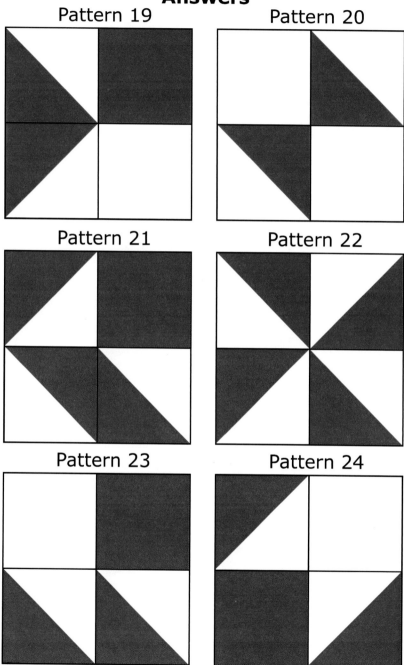

Block Design
Answers

Pattern 25

Pattern 26

Pattern 27

Pattern 28

Pattern 29

Pattern 30

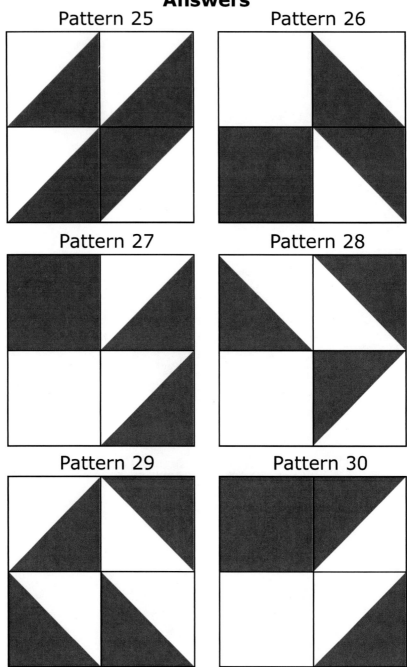

Block Design
Answers
Pattern 31

Pattern 32

Block Design
Answers
Pattern 33

Pattern 34

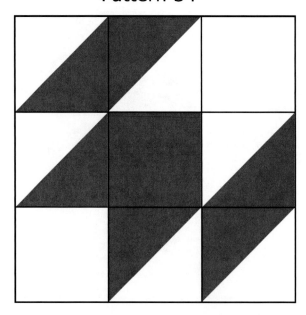

Block Design
Answers
Pattern 35

Pattern 36

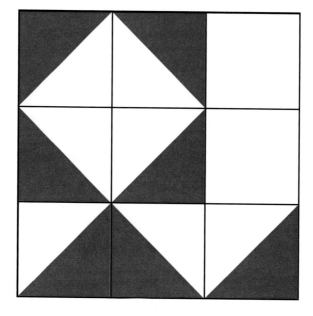

Block Design
Answers
Pattern 37

Pattern 38

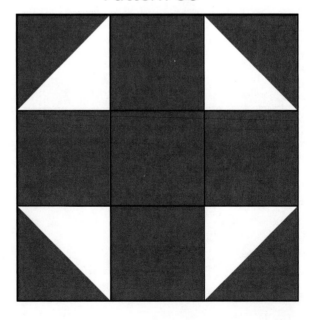

Block Design
Answers
Pattern 39

Pattern 40

Block Design
Answers

Pattern 41

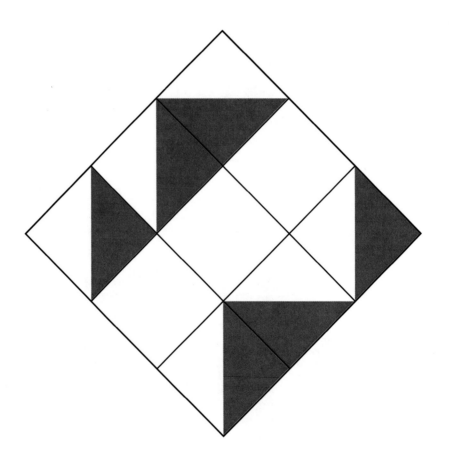

Block Design
Answers

Pattern 42

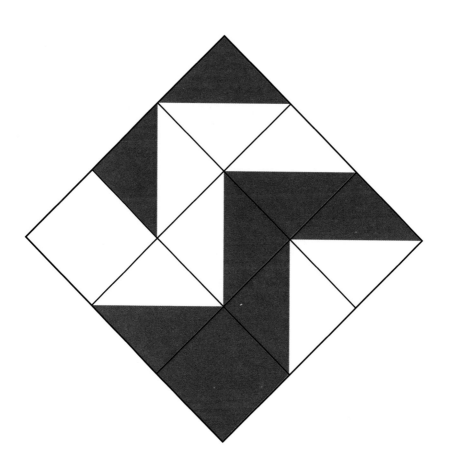

Block Design
Answers

Pattern 43

Block Design
Answers

Pattern 44

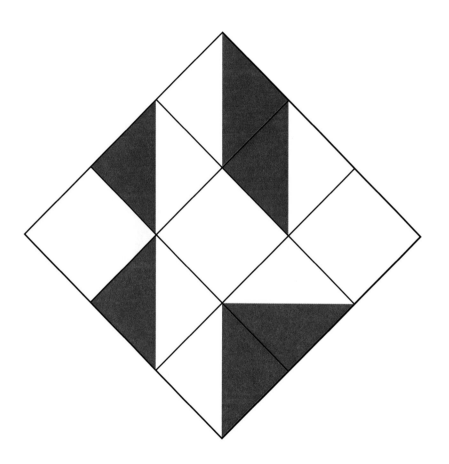

Block Design
Answers

Pattern 45

Block Design
Answers

Pattern 46

Block Design
Answers

Pattern 47

Block Design
Answers

Pattern 48

Block Design
Answers

Pattern 49

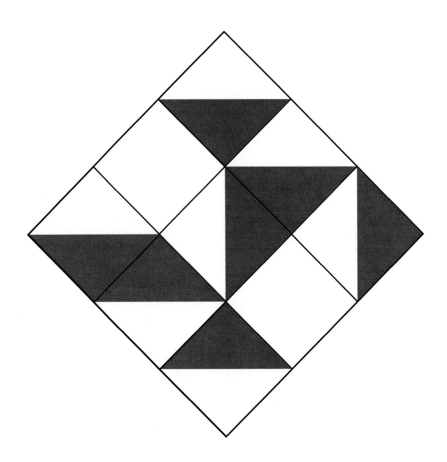

Block Design
Answers

Pattern 50

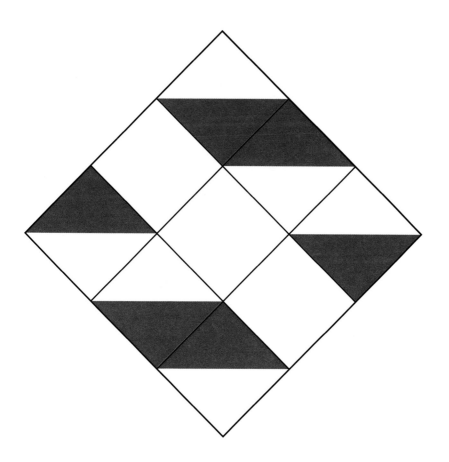

**Thank you for your purchase!
I hope you enjoyed this book!**

Please consider leaving a review!

Made in the USA
Las Vegas, NV
13 October 2023

79064731R00117